Calming Your Anxiety

Learn How to Use

Neuroscience to Manage

Panic, Worry, and Anxiety

Evana Grant

© Copyright 2020 - All rights reserved.

The content contained within this book may not be reproduced, duplicated or transmitted without direct written permission from the author or the publisher.

Under no circumstances will any blame or legal responsibility be held against the publisher, or author, for any damages, reparation, or monetary loss due to the information contained within this book, either directly or indirectly.

Legal Notice:

This book is copyright protected. It is only for personal use. You cannot amend, distribute, sell, use, quote or paraphrase any part, or the content within this book, without the consent of the author or publisher.

Disclaimer Notice:

Please note the information contained within this document is for educational and entertainment purposes only. All effort has been executed to present accurate, up to date, reliable, complete information. No warranties of any kind are declared or implied. Readers acknowledge that the author is not engaged in the rendering of legal, financial, medical or professional advice. The content within this book has been derived from various sources. Please consult a licensed professional before attempting any techniques outlined in this book.

By reading this document, the reader agrees that under no circumstances is the author responsible for any losses, direct or indirect, that are incurred as a result of the use of the information contained within this document, including, but not limited to, errors, omissions, or inaccuracies.

Table of Contents

INTRODUCTION 1

THERE ARE FIVE MAJOR ANXIETY DISORDERS 3
Generalized Anxiety Disorder 3
Panic Disorder 4
Social Anxiety (Also Known as Social Phobia) 5
Specific Phobias 6
Separation Anxiety Disorder (or SAD) 8
DETERMINE YOUR ANXIETY LEVEL 9

CHAPTER 1: DON'T BE ALOOF! 15

VOICE YOUR WORRIES AND CONCERNS 16
HOW TO APPROACH OTHERS AND SEEK HELP 17
BE SOCIALLY ACTIVE 21
Tips to Help You Prepare for a Social or Public Event 23
COMMIT TO A POSITIVE LIFESTYLE 24
Rewire Your Restless Mind 24
Surround Yourself With Positive People 25
ANXIETY AND RELATIONSHIPS 27
How to Weaken Your Anxiety and Fortify Your Relationship 32

CHAPTER 2: GO HEALTHY 37

GET ENOUGH SLEEP 37
Follow a Steady Sleep Routine 37
How Sleep Can Help Reduce Anxiety and Stress 39
Tips on Getting Yourself a Sound Night's Sleep 40
LIMIT CAFFEINE, ALCOHOL, AND NICOTINE INTAKE 41
The Link Between Psychotropic Drugs and Stress . 41
How Psychotropic Drugs Can Impact Your Body .. 42

Tips on How to Limit Your Intake of Psychotropic Drugs 43
EXERCISE REGULARLY 44
Endorphins and Mental Well-Being 44
Exercise Can Help Calm Anxiety 45
Tips on How to Commit to an Active Lifestyle 46
GO ON A HEALTHY DIET 48
Foods Than Help Reduce Anxiety 49
Link Between An Unhealthy Diet and Anxiety Disorder 52

CHAPTER 3: STRESS MANAGEMENT 53

SIGNS OF STRESS 54
WHICH SITUATIONS MAKE YOU MOST ANXIOUS? 55
Identify Your Personal Triggers 56
How to Manage Your Stress 59
PUT AN END TO CHRONIC NERVOUSNESS AND UNEASINESS 62
Acknowledge, Confront, and Reflect on Your Fears 63
Guided Self-Meditation to Ease Your Worries and Fears 66

CHAPTER 4: RELAXING TECHNIQUES 69

BREATHING TECHNIQUES 69
Different Breathing Exercises to Try 70
How Breathing Can Help Your Body Relax 73
PRACTICING MINDFULNESS 75
What is Mindfulness? How Can It Help Reduce Anxiety? 75
How to Practice Mindfulness 79
MEDITATION 81
How Meditation Helps in Reducing Anxiety 82
Types of Meditation to Practice 83
Links to Guided Meditation and Meditation Music 88

CHAPTER 5: ANXIETY RELAPSES 89

DIFFERENCE BETWEEN A LAPSE AND A RELAPSE 89
HOW TO AVOID A RELAPSE 90
BREAKING BAD HABITS 94

Chart to Identify Bad Habits and Ways to Overcome Them.. 98

CHAPTER 6: THERAPY AND MEDICATION 99

WHEN TO SEEK PROFESSIONAL HELP? 100
THERAPY 101
Cognitive Behavioral Therapy (CBT) 101
Exposure Therapy 106
PRESCRIBED MEDICATION 110
Types of Different Anxiety Medication 110
MARIJUANA AND CBD 113
CBD and THC 114
How CBD Works 116
Is Cannabis Safe? 116
Is CBD Safe? 117
OTHER HOLISTIC THERAPIES 118
Traditional Chinese Medicine 118
Tibetan Medicine 119
Hypnotherapy 121
Aromatherapy 122
Botanical Remedies 124

CHAPTER 7: CLOSING REFLECTION 129

TESTIMONIAL 129
SETTING YOUR GOALS 132
14 Reasons Why Focused Goal Setting Is Important: 134
How to Set Your Goals 135
SELF-REFLECTION IS VITAL FOR A POSITIVE ATTITUDE 137
Reflection Chart 138

CONCLUSION 141

A PREVENTATIVE PROTECTION PLAN 141
FINAL WORD 144

REFERENCES 147

Introduction

Have you ever felt uneasy and agitated and did not know why? Do you have constant worries that others find irrational? Do you feel fearful before an exam or a job interview? Does it make you feel restless? Does your body react in a certain way when you feel fearful and nervous? Well, that's what anxiety is, whether your symptoms are severe or mild, chronic or sporadic. **Anxiety** is the body's response to the *perception* of danger; that is how you respond physically, mentally, and emotionally to a perceived danger. This danger is probably unreal and irrational; however, it hovers over your mind, and in many cases, this fear becomes constant and will probably affect your daily life. Stress and past traumatic events play a major role in causing chronic anxiety, even if the body does not react to these situations at the time of happening.

This e-book will introduce you first to what anxiety is, how it feels, and the major types of anxiety disorders. The purpose of this book is to help you identify what you're going through and help you find the right ways to deal with your anxiety disorder. Anxiety affects our lives in many ways, especially when it comes to our relationships, social life, and work. Thus, this e-book will help you to get out of your solitude, aid you to live a healthy lifestyle, teach you to connect with your surroundings, help you to manage your stress, and introduce you to different methods of meditation. All of these will build your fortitude and assist you to become your own therapist.

There are many types of anxiety disorders, but the most general one is generalized anxiety disorder (GAD). GAD is the incessant and extreme worry about several situations. Those with GAD, for example, may feel apprehensive and await disaster and may be excessively fretful about daily issues such as work, money, family, health, specific events, or other matters. These people cannot control their worry, and it usually clouds their judgment and affects their decisions. The most common physical reactions to GAD may be characterized by feeling irritable and uneasy for a prolonged period of time, with the constant feeling of impending danger. This may cause the heart rate to increase, along with rapid breathing, hyperventilating, sweating, and trembling. This, of course, causes the person with GAD to feel weak and tired most of the time, probably due to lack of sleep, and thus making it difficult to concentrate on certain tasks. Many people with anxiety disorders also experience gastrointestinal (GI) problems as well, which in turn causes them abdominal and stomach aches.

There Are Five Major Anxiety Disorders

Generalized Anxiety Disorder

Like mentioned earlier, individuals with GAD feel uneasy and fearful about different things for a long period of time (six months or more). They may experience the constant feeling of being anxious and apprehensive, not only in particular stressful situations such an exam or a job interview. These worries become persistent and extreme, and thus may interrupt their normal lives. Trivial daily triggers, such as running a certain errand or attending a social event, may lead to an overwhelming worry and a feeling that something horrific will happen.

In some cases, GAD may be accompanied by other disorders such as social phobia, depression, OCD, or PTSD. People with severe anxiety may be subjected to alcohol or drug abuse and could suffer from a variety of physical health issues such as headaches (or migraines), muscle tension, or bowel conditions.

Panic Disorder

Panic disorder is characterized as an anxiety disorder in which you frequently experience panic attacks. It is common for anyone to feel anxious and fearful since it's our body's natural response to stressful events and/or dangerous situations. However, those with panic disorder feel anxious, stressed, scared, and uneasy frequently, and most of the time the cause of these feelings is irrational, even unapparent.

The main symptom of panic disorder is anxiety, which can cause a person to evade certain events or situations because they may initiate an attack. Thus, the cycle of fear becomes overwhelming, and may cause the person to have more attacks. During a panic attack, a person experiences a flash of severe mental as well as physical symptoms. This may happen rapidly and for no evident reason, causing what seems to be close to a heart attack: increase in heart rate, difficulty breathing, chest pain, feeling weak (some may feel they are about to faint), sweating, nausea, tingling or numbness, and dryness in the mouth.

Panic attacks may be fear-provoking and painful, but they are not dangerous or life-threatening. Most panic attacks last five to 20 minutes, but some may go on up to an hour. Some may experience panic attacks on a weekly basis, others every month or two, depending on the level of daily stressors.

Social Anxiety (Also Known as Social Phobia)

Those who suffer from social anxiety disorder experience extreme anxiety and fear over being judged negatively, scrutinized harshly, embarrassed, and excluded in social or public events. People with social anxiety disorder have a constant worry about their anxiety being obvious, which may cause them to blush or stutter. For example, they would fear going up stage to present or give a speech, worrying that they might be laughed at or judged as being awkward or uninteresting.

Therefore, they often dodge social or public events, for it may cause them a lot of distress. The most common symptoms of social anxiety disorder are rapid heart rate, sweating, and vomiting, and in many cases, it may trigger panic attacks. Social anxiety can be overwhelming and uncontrollable, even if the person does acknowledge that the feeling of fear and worry is unreasonable.

Specific Phobias

You may hate being in closed places, like an elevator, or high places like the roof of a building or a bridge. This would most probably make you feel discomfort or even scared, but this can only be momentary and would not impact your lifestyle or daily decisions.

However, if you have a specific phobia, the feeling of fear is so intense that it may cause a lot of distress. For example, if you have seismophobia (fear of earthquakes), then you'd feel uneasy leaving your comfort zone. You would have a constant fear that an earthquake may hit at any time, and you'd have the urgent need to secure a safe place. This can be overwhelming, for it may stop you from going to places, sleeping restfully, and concentrating at tasks. Being phobic may lower your self-esteem and can disturb your daily routine. It may also affect your work productivity and social interactions, as well as cause tension in your relationships. While some phobias develop in childhood, most seem to arise unexpectedly, usually during adolescence or early adulthood. Thus, people who experience extreme and irrational fears in the presence of or in anticipation of a specific object or event have a specific phobia.

Ten most common specific phobias:

- Social phobia
- Agoraphobia (fear of being alone and not finding an escape)
- Claustrophobia (fear of being trapped in closed spaces)
- Acrophobia (fear of heights)
- Hypochondria (fear of becoming ill)
- Arachnophobia (fear of spiders)
- Mysophobia (fear of germs)
- Aerophobia (fear of flying)
- Trypanophobia (fear of needles and injections)
- Ophidiophobia (fear of snakes)

Most phobias start at an early age, due to experiencing a traumatic event or a stressful situation. In some cases, children may develop a phobia because one of the parents has a phobia and the child learns it.

Separation Anxiety Disorder (or SAD)

SAD is mostly common in babies and children, and it's a natural aspect of child development. However, it can still occur in adults. It is identified as the fear of separation from a parent or loved one. For babies and children, this can cause anxiety and odd behavior such as too much clinging to parent(s), severe crying upon slightest separation, aggressive emotional tantrums (may include vomiting), nightmares, rejecting sleeping alone, and weak performance at school. SAD is most commonly caused due a family's history of anxiety, depression or other mental illness, divorce, overprotective parents, moving to a new setting or school, or the death of a close loved one.

As for adults with SAD, they may have the constant fear and worry of losing a close loved one or a pet. If you have SAD, then you most probably feel an abnormal distress upon separating from a person close to you, excessive worry that the other person may be harmed and thus separated from you, and extreme apprehension about being alone. This may affect your daily routine and decisions, for it would affect your relationship with this person as you would tend to be overprotective, controlling, officious, and even judgmental. For instance, if your spouse tells that he or she will be late coming home, you'd feel anxious and jump into negative conclusions such as your spouse not wanting to spend time with you.

An adult may develop severe anxiety as a result of the separation, and this may also be manifested in physical symptoms such as headaches, vomiting, and/or trembling.

Determine Your Anxiety Level

Take the following quiz to determine the level of your anxiety. Consider your emotional state in the past few months, and choose the answer that best describes each of the following anxiety symptoms.

1. Increased heart rate/Pounding heart beats

1) Not at all   2) Rarely   3) Sometimes   4) Frequently   5) Always

2. Sweating

1) Not at all   2) Rarely   3) Sometimes   4) Frequently   5) Always

3. Trembling of hands/numbness

1) Not at all   2) Rarely   3) Sometimes   4) Frequently   5) Always

4. Constant Fear

1) Not at all   2) Rarely   3) Sometimes   4) Frequently   5) Always

5. Chest pain and difficulty in breathing

1) Not at all   2) Rarely   3) Sometimes   4) Frequently   5) Always

6. Nausea or stomach ache

1) Not at all   2) Rarely   3) Sometimes   4) Frequently   5) Always

7. Feeling dizzy or light-headed

1) Not at all   2) Rarely   3) Sometimes   4) Frequently   5) Always

8. Fear of losing control

1) Not at all   2) Rarely   3) Sometimes   4) Frequently   5) Always

9. Fear of embarrassment and humiliation

1) Not at all   2) Rarely   3) Sometimes   4) Frequently   5) Always

10. Fear of dying

1) Not at all   2) Rarely   3) Sometimes   4) Frequently   5) Always

11. Relentless worry

1) Not at all   2) Rarely   3) Sometimes   4) Frequently   5) Always

12. Inability to focus on a specific task

1) Not at all   2) Rarely   3) Sometimes   4) Frequently   5) Always

13. Inability to relax/Restlessness

1) Not at all   2) Rarely   3) Sometimes   4) Frequently   5) Always

14. Feeling of being unreal/out of it

1) Not at all   2) Rarely   3) Sometimes   4) Frequently   5) Always

15. Feeling of nervousness and irritability

1) Not at all   2) Rarely   3) Sometimes   4) Frequently   5) Always

16. Difficulty in falling asleep

1) Not at all   2) Rarely   3) Sometimes   4) Frequently   5) Always

17. Headaches

1) Not at all   2) Rarely   3) Sometimes   4) Frequently   5) Always

18. Avoiding social events due to worry and fear

1) Not at all   2) Rarely   3) Sometimes   4) Frequently   5) Always

19. Feeling lethargic and out of energy

1) Not at all   2) Rarely   3) Sometimes   4) Frequently   5) Always

20. Preferring to be alone

1) Not at all   2) Rarely   3) Sometimes   4) Frequently   5) Always

21. Feeling agitated

1) Not at all   2) Rarely   3) Sometimes   4) Frequently   5) Always

22. Muscle tension

1) Not at all   2) Rarely   3) Sometimes   4) Frequently   5) Always

Calculate Your Result

Sum up your score on your responses (as indicated by the number preceding them). Scores will range from 22 to 110

22-35 points: You don't have anxiety, you are free of worries!

Your answers suggest that you most likely do not suffer from any anxiety disorders. You may have some little worries that cause you occasional feelings of anxiety in your life. The low range of your result may indicate that you feel detached from your surroundings, which isn't very healthy, and you should work on helping yourself to become reattached to those around you. Follow the instructions given in this book and practice the healthy habits provided such as mindfulness, meditation, and exercise!

36-50 points: You do experience mild anxiety, nothing major.

Your answers to this anxiety assessment indicate that at the present time, you probably face some stressful situations, but do not suffer from any major anxiety disorders. The anxiety you experience is completely normal; we face stressful circumstances every day and it's a part of our life. It's only natural to experience some anxiety, as it is our body's method of informing us that we should pay closer attention to our mental and physical health, situations surrounding us, and the people involved in our lives. Your result implies you have an average level of anxiety, but it doesn't mean that you can be diagnosed with an anxiety disorder. Practice some daily techniques for relaxation as suggested in this book to help you cope with daily stress.

51-70 points: Your anxiety is moderate. You can work on it!

Your replies to this anxiety assessment indicate that you may be experiencing moderate anxiety and you may be diagnosed with an anxiety disorder. You should listen to your body and recognize your symptoms. Pay attention to your symptoms and take notice of the situations or the triggers that cause you to be anxious. This is neither a diagnosis or a call for treatment. Nonetheless, it is best to practice the different meditation techniques and healthy lifestyle tips recommended in this book. If you want to seek a specific diagnosis for your anxiety, then you should visit a specialized doctor.

71-110: You suffer from severe anxiety. Stay the healing process!

According to your result of this anxiety assessment, you most probably suffer from an anxiety disorder. The responses you've given indicate that you face intense anxiety symptoms. This is not a diagnosis nor a call for a treatment, but you shouldn't take this lightly. It is recommended to visit a specialized doctor and inquire about your possible disorder. Follow the instructions and tips in this book and practice the different relaxation methods as well as the healthy lifestyle tips to alleviate your anxiety symptoms.

Chapter 1:
Don't Be Aloof!

People with anxiety usually tend to isolate themselves and avoid any social interactions or events. A lot of people feel anxious but they can't comprehend what they're feeling, especially if the cause of their fears and worries is unspecified. Thus they find themselves unable to understand themselves or to explain how they feel to others. Many mistake anxiety for depression, especially if it lasts for a long period of time.

As adolescents undergo any kind of emotional affliction or distressing situation, they usually feel anxious and tend to harshly pity or criticize themselves. Young adults may find themselves unable to adapt to certain conditions, such as the inability to make friends, and most of the time think that there's something wrong with them. Therefore, they withdraw from their surroundings and find comfort in solitude. This also causes them low self-esteem, which will ultimately build a timid personality.

Being aloof is never the answer. Even if you feel that no one understands you, be sure that someone does. There are several ways to help you connect with your surroundings to be able to seek help and find solutions for your anxiety.

Voice Your Worries and Concerns

It's definitely not the easiest thing to open up to others and explain to them what you're feeling. You'd probably ask yourself many times whether you should talk to a loved one about your feelings of fear and worry, but many of us can't find the courage, words, or trust to do so. It's vital to find someone that you can really trust and know that they won't be judgmental or misunderstand what you're going through. It usually takes a single step to just voice out how you feel, why you feel that way, and what kind of help you expect; that's why it is fundamental that you reflect on your emotions and mental state and try to understand yourself first.

If you are unable to understand your anxious behavior, you can simply monitor how your body responds to your feelings. We may think that anxiety stems from our minds, but in fact it's a physical response to "your perception" of danger. Next time you feel that you have a rapid heart rate, difficulty breathing, sweating, or tingling in the palms and/or arms, ask yourself what kind of feeling you are experiencing as your body is reacting in that way. This is what anxiety generally feels like, and in most cases when you're feeling anxious, you may not know what is causing you this uneasy feeling. This is because anxiety may hit hours or days after you have witnessed a certain distressing event, or maybe accumulated stress and negative emotions. Perhaps you need to take notes and try to explain using words how you are feeling and how your body is reacting to your emotions.

How to Approach Others and Seek Help

It is indeed challenging to inform and explain to others about an anxiety disorder. An important step is to plan ahead and know what words you're going to use to describe the emotions you feel inside. Consider the following suggestions which can help you feel comfortable and confident to open up to a close one and seek help.

- It is beneficial to jot down your thoughts and plan ahead. Writing and wording your emotions can help you organize and simplify your thoughts.
- Try to research your disorder and write down ideas that you think are relevant to you. This will help you first to understand more about your disorder, and then to be able to explain it clearly to others. You should also think of what aspects about the disorder you want to speak about and which ones you believe you should keep to yourself.
- Consider why you want to open up and tell your trusted one about your anxiety disorder. Are you expecting this person to help you? Or do you just need someone to listen to you?
- If you are seeking help, make sure that you are specific and clear. Being vague won't help the other person understand what you're going through.
- Do not consider your disorder a weakness. In fact, opening up to others is a sign of great strength and courage.
- It would be a good idea to find information about your disorder and share it with the other person. It's good to explain how you feel in your own words, but it'll also make you feel

more confident as you are credible by supporting what you're saying with medical evidence.
- You should definitely consider several responses or reactions from the person. Make sure you tell them that you do not expect pity but understanding. Prepare yourself to different reactions and what you would say in response.
- Make sure to set up the right time and place to approach your trusted person. It's important that you be considerate to the person's emotional state and their preparedness to learn about your disorder. Be prepared and don't back down if you feel anxious.
- If the person's reaction isn't as you've planned, don't give up. You shouldn't expect everyone to understand about your disorder. However, be sure that you can always find support in people who may share similar or other disorders. Maybe other people's experiences can be helpful to you.
- Finally, remember not to be fully dependent on others. You should respect other people's emotional well-being and be in control of your own state of mind and emotions.

Be Socially Active

Many people with anxiety, especially social anxiety, grow tense or self-conscious when being out in public or in certain situations, like attending a party, going on a date, applying for a new job, or maybe giving a speech to an audience. Some may mistake this for being timid or lacking self-esteem, but social anxiety disorder encompasses extreme dread of social circumstances, particularly circumstances that are new and strange to you, for you may feel as if you're being watched or scrutinized by others. In such situations, you may feel fearful and anxious. This may get you to avoid others, hence disrupting your social life.

Being self-conscious is the constant worry of being evaluated, judged, or embarrassed publicly. Negative thoughts hover in your mind, and you fear that people will think badly of you or think you're not as valuable as others. Though you may know that your fear of being judged is unreasonable and exaggerated, you still can't control your anxiety. However, you can teach yourself to be at ease in social events and get your life back on track.

You probably assume that you're the only one who gets socially awkward and shy. The fact is social anxiety is rather common, but the triggers may differ. For some, social anxiety is linked to social events like public speeches or performing on stage, while others may feel anxious by meeting new people or even making a small talk with others. Basically, it's the feeling that you are the center of attention and an object of scrutiny that makes people mostly anxious and self-conscious.

Staying aloof and anti-social is not the answer. You should gradually face your fears and challenge yourself to go out. The first step is to challenge your mentality and shut down the negative thoughts that cross your mind and hinder your ability to be comfortably sociable. Stop telling yourself that you may embarrass yourself or end up like a fool. Don't let the voice in your head convince you that you will be tongue-tied or shy. Instead, tell yourself that you can be confident, you can start a conversation, and you can show others what you're all about. It's important that you identify these automatic negative thoughts that make you fearful, and once you do, you can evaluate these thoughts and try to validate whether they are rational or not. When you acknowledge that your fear and worry are irrational and only fuel your anxiety, then you can help yourself to shut them down. Eliminating these negative thoughts is definitely effective and will help you minimize the signs of social anxiety.

Tips to Help You Prepare for a Social or Public Event

- Think of yourself and not others. It only matters how you value yourself and now how others see you.
- Don't assume that things will go wrong because this will get you anxious even before going. Set your mentality on the notion that you want to have fun and enjoy your time.
- If you get nervous, so what? Take a minute by yourself to take a few breaths.
- Don't assume that you'll be the center of attention. At social events, people want to enjoy their time and it's not really all about you!
- Focus your attention on other people and not yourself. Think of what interests them, and maybe that can be an icebreaker. Let your focus be external and not internal.
- Don't pressure yourself to be perfect; no one really is!
- Enjoy the moment. Don't spend your time worrying about what's next and how it'll turn out to be.

Commit to a Positive Lifestyle

Rewire Your Restless Mind

Whenever you feel panicked or anxious, your mind gets alert and does not comprehend the source of this panic because the body is responding to the perception of danger, but there's no apparent danger. It's advised to change your habitual action. For example, if you're sleeping and feel panicked, get up and let your body and mind know that you're pulling away from the threat that you're feeling. Consider having an anchor thought (a positive stimulating thought that pulls you out of your present mindset). For example, think of a happy place where you feel secure, happy, and fortified. Visualize this place and let it be your mind's sanctuary. By doing this, you're activating the part of your brain that works when making cognitive decisions (prefrontal cortex). Your mind will now respond to a happy stimulus and in turn send a message to your body to calm down.

It's not a complicated process to rewire your restless mind. Actually, scientists call this 'neuroplasticity.' In other words, your brain has the ability to constantly rewire itself and adjust itself to new situations. But to be able to rewire your brain, you must consciously make a decision to rewire your thoughts and make them more positive.

What you need to do first is change your mindset. Start the minute you wake up in the morning. Don't sulk in bed and go over negative thoughts that stifle your body and mind. Instead, get up and do a certain activity, whether physical and mental, like playing a game or going for a jog. Boost your mind with positivity and consciously think of positive and happy things or places.

Surround Yourself With Positive People

People around you will either motivate or wreck you. Believe it or not, we are much more influenced by those around us than we would like to believe. That's why it is fundamental to surround yourself with people who will lift you up and not drag you down. Surrounding yourself with optimistic and happy people will reflect on you and make you more positive, confident, and successful.

Don't be afraid to let go of negative and passive people from your life. There's no shame in deciding to eliminate that kind of negativity from your life. Instead, find people that inspire, encourage, and boost your confidence. Negative people are toxic and will definitely influence your mindset negatively. Don't put a lot of emphasis on this kind of people and don't value their opinion much. You surely don't have to cut them completely off your life, especially if they are close family members or lifelong friends, but you can at least limit the time you spend with them. Use your time efficiently and choose the people that will bring joy to your life and not those who bring unneeded drama.

It won't be too hard to tell the difference between positive and negative people. Positive people are winners—people who are successful and choose to progress and develop continually. Keep in mind that those who really care about you will work to bring out the best of you.

Anxiety and Relationships

Unfortunately, anxiety does not only impact the physical, mental, and emotional health, but it can shake relationships as well. Anxiety tends to cause a lot of tension and can significantly influence your thoughts. If you feel that you're struggling in your relationship, then anxiety must be playing its part. Here's how anxiety can put your relationship at risk:

- Anxiety can make you feel fearful and worried about the future, which causes you to neglect your needs as well as your partner's needs. When you worry about what may happen in the future, then you are disregarding what is happening at the present moment. This overwhelming feeling will reflect on your partner as well, which will cause a strain on your relationship. Your brain might escape what's happening in the present and stray into irrational thoughts which may cloud your judgment. That's why you need to train your mind into only considering the moment and not worry too much about what may happen in the future. Unfortunately, this may break the trust and connection with your partner due to your withdrawal, misjudgment of situations, or anger bursts.

- When you are experiencing anxiety, you may find it hard to express your true feelings. This will probably make you suppress your thoughts and emotions, which is not healthy because then you will harbor negative emotions and your thoughts will be tainted with irrationality. Hence, anxiety will get worse and eventually get out of control. This will cause anger bursts or aggressive defensive behavior.

- Anxiety may cause you to focus all your attention on your own concerns and problems, and neglect what your partner is experiencing or feeling. This will lead to selfish behavior from your part because you will feel the need to be defensive. These negative feelings will become contagious. Eventually, resentment and tension will be built up in the relationship.

- Most of the time anxiety makes you feel inept and stuck. This feeling of hopelessness will make you avoid taking healthy and beneficial decisions that would make a positive change in your life. Remember, anxiety is the opposite of acceptance; you will no longer feel comfortable to take the right decisions, which may frustrate your partner and strain him/her.

- When you are anxious, you are unhappy, mainly because you lack the feeling of being safe and free. Instead, you feel worried, fearful, and constrained. You will no longer be able to enjoy intimacy and sex. Destructive thoughts and qualms will distract you and prevent you from being existent within a relationship, which will suck out the pleasure of a moment.

- People who experience anxiety are in constant need of reassurance to feel safe and secure. This can be especially arduous to your partner. Your persistent demand for reassurance might drain out your partner's emotions, causing them to limit their communication with you, and they may choose to withdraw.

- Insecurity may lead you to feel constant worry about being abandoned by your partner. You will feel vulnerable as you can't control or secure what your partner is feeling or thinking. Feeling out of control can inflict chaotic and restless thoughts. This will cloud your judgment and cause you to be in constant doubt of being loved and worry about being abandoned.

- When you're anxious, you tend to send mixed signals to your partner. The surge of emotions and thoughts will make you demand different things from your partner. For example, you may feel exhausted and down at one moment, wanting to be alone. However, the next moment you'd feel insecure and worried and ask for reassurance and comfort. These mixed signals may cause your partner to feel perplexed and even overwhelmed.

How to Weaken Your Anxiety and Fortify Your Relationship

When you recognize and understand how anxiety affects your relationship, you can create positive changes to make your relationship more vibrant. It's essential to build trust with your partner in order to reduce the power anxiety has over you. Consider the following tips that can help you weaken your anxiety and fortify your relationship:

- Practice mindfulness. That is, live in the moment. This will be discussed further in chapter 4. If your mind keeps on straying to thoughts about the future or the past, focus your attention to the present moment. Communicate openly what you're feeling with your partner instead of withdrawing or suppressing your emotions.
- Do not suppress your thoughts and emotions. You first have to think rationally and recognize the thoughts that drain your emotions and

energy. Then, approach your partner calmly and address the issues that need to be dealt with.

- Consider your needs and not your fears. When you find yourself turning apprehensive or defensive, stop and remember the love you have for yourself and your partner. Let your partner know that you are sorry for being self-absorbed and not paying attention to their needs.

- Give yourself confidence. Remember, you reflect your emotions and attitudes on your partner. Your partner wants to see you happy and comfortable; allow yourself to feel that so you can live contentedly with your loved one.

- Don't take yourself too seriously. One way to deal with being anxious is to enjoy some sense of humor. Be determined to laugh, play, and enjoy the moment with your partner. Joyfulness has a physical effect on you and comforts your brain, leading to a dynamic and healthy relationship.

- It's perfectly okay to be uncertain about what your partner is thinking and feeling. You don't have to always be reassured that you are loved. Endure this kind of discomfort; as you practice this, you will gradually feel fulfilled and reduce the need to feel reassured at all times.
- Remember, you are not your thoughts. You can control your thoughts as you notice your thought stream. Paying conscious attention to your thoughts allows you to examine whether they are true, accurate, and rational.
- Accept your emotions. Being in a relationship includes many ups and downs. Cherish the ups and embrace the downs. Find ways to soothe yourself when feeling hurt, angered, or worried. It's only natural to feel vulnerable when being in love; this closeness with another person will naturally bring a series of emotions. Accept these emotions and don't just throw them at

your partner. Deal with your emotions first and then approach your partner for help.

- Communication is always the key. Your partner won't be able to understand you if you don't share your emotions and concerns with them. As you voice your concerns, make sure to listen to what your partner has to say as well. Your partner might have their own issues that they need to communicate with you.

- Acknowledge when anxiety affects your attitude and communicate this with your partner. It's ok to say, "I get overwhelmed and anxious sometimes; it makes me overreact." Be true to yourself, and if you feel you need more attention, simply ask for it.

- Your partner is not your complaint box. This will definitely make them feel emotionally drained. Don't rely on your partner to solve your issues, simply because they might not know how. If you're feeling too swamped with your thoughts and emotions, consider seeing a therapist.

Chapter 2:
Go Healthy

Get Enough Sleep

Follow a Steady Sleep Routine

Anxiety disorders are often linked to sleep deprivation. It's only normal for someone who is excessively worried and fearful to find it hard to fall asleep or stay asleep throughout the night. Insomnia, along with anxiety, can cause negative implications for overall health. Therefore, it is essential to understand the link between anxiety and sleep to be able to tackle it appropriately.

Our brain is responsible for our mental health; studies have shown that lack of sleep is detrimental and affects the brain. Doctors recommend seven to nine hours of sleep every night, which will definitely help rewire the brain and heal your mental and emotional problems (Suni, E. 2019).

It is vital to commit yourself to a sleeping routine. You should start by scheduling an optimal bedtime which will provide you with seven to nine sleeping hours every night. For instance, if you have to wake up early to work, perhaps at 7:00 a.m., then you should probably hit the sack by no later than 11:00 p.m.

It would be a good idea to have a reminder, whether on your phone or smart watch, to get you to bed. It's fundamental to follow the same schedule every night so your sleeping hours won't be disrupted. Make sure to reset your alarm for the morning!

Once you find yourself waking up before your alarm rings in the morning, then you can be sure of your optimal bed timing. However, if you find yourself too sleepy to wake up and tend to snooze the alarm more than once, then maybe you should go to sleep 15 to 30 minutes earlier at night.

How Sleep Can Help Reduce Anxiety and Stress

Insomnia is a common symptom of anxiety disorders due to the fact that once you put your head on your pillow, you tend to ruminate about your concerns; this gets you anxious and deprives you from falling asleep.

Insomnia in turn causes distress and can make anxiety even worse. The worry about being unable to feel asleep will make a person more anxious and worried.

Sleep deprivation affects the overall emotional and mental health, which can aggravate the challenges presented by anxiety disorders. This negative cycle can be self-induced: anxiety causes poor sleep, causing you to have more severe anxiety and more sleep troubles.

Sleep is potent in reducing anxiety and stress. Committing to a steady sleep routine helps the body and mind to relax and heal gradually. It also increases your ability to concentrate and also enhances your mood. Sleep helps you to think more clearly, to make conscious decisions, and to solve your problems easily.

Research shows that lack of sleep makes you more irritable, more stressed, and more vulnerable to negative spurs; this may affect your relationships as well as your performance at school or workplace.

Tips on Getting Yourself a Sound Night's Sleep

As established earlier, there's a close link between anxiety and sleep. Thus, once you build healthy sleeping habits, you will find that you are less stressed during the day.

Here are some tips for a better sleep hygiene:

- Make your bed more comfortable and eliminate any sources of sleep disruption, like light and noise.
- Turn off all electronic devices, such as TVs, computers, and smartphones.
- Avoid large meals, caffeine, and alcohol before bedtime.
- Try relaxation techniques which can help you calm down and fall asleep quickly and easily.
- Practice deep breathing, mindfulness meditation, and guided imagery; these are

available for free online, and they can help put your mind calm down before bed.
- Exercise in the afternoon or in the evening. Your body will release the negative energy and relax, and this will help you sleep more easily at night.

Limit Caffeine, Alcohol, and Nicotine Intake

The Link Between Psychotropic Drugs and Stress

Caffeine, alcohol, and nicotine are the most common psychotropic drugs. People without health issues consume them regularly, but these can create dependence, and in case of addiction, they tend to cause acute and chronic mental disorders.

Caffeine can play the role of the enemy of your body. Studies show that excessive intake of caffeine increases risk of anxiety, especially panic attacks. Both caffeine and nicotine play a role in stimulating anxiety in different ways, particularly by subsidizing the physiological arousal associated with anxiety.

How Psychotropic Drugs Can Impact Your Body

Caffeine may impact anxiety by its action on specific receptors and neurotransmitters in the brain, which in turn trigger and exacerbate anxiety. Caffeine can induce neuroendocrine stress response systems through its effects on the stress hormone cortisol in the body, which stimulates the flight-or-fight response that causes anxiety or panic symptoms.

Regular smokers consider smoking a habit that alleviates anxiety and that's why they continue to smoke, especially when feeling stressed. The truth is, smoking does not calm your anxiety but relieves your nicotine withdrawal symptoms. This relief only lasts for 30 minutes or so, but when the craving for another cigarette starts, the anxiety returns.

Alcohol and nicotine are widely consumed due to the fact that they have become social habits. Smoking a cigarette and drinking alcohol may give you a temporary relief from your stress, but you have to be careful because they have paradoxical effects on the body. They contribute to both conserving and deteriorating anxiety symptoms.

Alcohol is a depressant and can provide a calming, sedative effect to the body when consumed. However, consuming alcohol over a long period of time can make your anxiety even worse due to the withdrawal symptoms that are very much like the symptoms of anxiety and panic attacks.

It's good to keep in mind that even though psychotropic drugs provide instant yet temporary relief, they can also mess up your mind. Alcohol abuse can have clear physical and mental effects. Consuming too much alcohol may cause your body to collapse, even suffer memory loss or brain damage.

Tips on How to Limit Your Intake of Psychotropic Drugs

- Most people can't start their day without a nice cup of coffee. A cup a day won't do you any harm, but if you're a coffee addict, then you should find other alternatives. Try decaffeinated coffee or other herbal teas. Herbal tea (chamomile, for example) can help your mind relax and soothe your anxiety.
- Reduce your alcohol intake and limit it to social events if you have to. Drinking moderately (around once a week) won't do much damage, but if you have an alcohol addiction, then you

must seek help or plan to reduce your alcohol consumption.
- Smoking is addictive, and it's definitely not easy to go cold turkey.
- Your brain is dependent on nicotine, and if you go without it, you will suffer the withdrawal symptoms. Maybe you should consider quit-smoking classes and apps, professional counseling, hypnosis, or at the least find a support group.

Exercise Regularly

Exercising, whether alone or in a group, is a helpful method to release negative energy and calm your anxiety. Sports do not only distract you from your anxious mind, but they also benefit you physically and biologically.

Endorphins and Mental Well-Being

Endorphins, or feel-good chemicals, are chemicals that are naturally produced by the nervous system to manage pain or stress. They are responsible for easing pain and boosting energy and happiness.

Endorphins are mainly released in the hypothalamus and pituitary glands. When you exercise vigorously, you have this sudden rush of positive energy; this is due to the increase of endorphin levels. The level of endorphins in the body differ from person to person. Research shows a link between low levels of endorphins and depression; that's why doctors advise people with depression and/or anxiety to exercise regularly in order to increase the level of endorphins in their bodies.

Exercise Can Help Calm Anxiety

Exercising does not only benefit your physical health, but your mental health as well. When you are physically active, chemicals are released in your brain that elevate your mood, as well as improving your memory. Moreover, exercising reduces muscle stiffness and hence relaxes your muscles and your feeling of anxiety.

Studies show that when you exercise, your increased heart rate affects brain chemistry, increasing the availability of important anti-anxiety neurochemicals such as serotonin (Steimer, 2002).

The amygdala is our body's reacting system to real or perceived threats or danger, which are the emotions that trigger anxiety. When you exercise, your brain's front region is activated and hence controls the amygdala. Research assures that a single exercise can help ease anxiety when it hits.

People with anxiety witnessed progress despite the type of activity they tried, whether high or low intensity exercises. No matter which activity you choose to do, what matters is that you don't give up and keep on trying to receive the best results. Last but not least, exercising, especially outdoor sports or group sports, boosts your social life and gets you out of solitude.

Tips on How to Commit to an Active Lifestyle

- *Follow your intrinsic motivation.* The trick is to do something you actually like and enjoy, without setting a specific reward or incentive. For instance, if you like nature, then start a walking program and do so with the mindset of simply employing your time in something that is enjoyable. You can start with 15 to 20 minutes a day and then increase the time as you find it suitable. Let the physical activity be something that would motivate and not burden you.
- *Develop an internal locus of control.* That is, put yourself in the mindset that you are in control of everything. When you choose the kind of activity that you like, then you are in control of

it. How you perceive yourself, whether in control or not, is the path your life is going to take. Thus, let the control be from within and not from any external forces. For example, if you like action sports or activities, join a martial arts class. This would be something that you control, enjoy, and learn certain skills from. The most important thing is not to procrastinate. Be in control of your time!

- *Set ultra easy goals!* Though the main aim of your activity is not to receive a reward other than enjoying the activity itself, a challenge is always vital. However, you shouldn't set unachievable goals for yourself because this will make you give up easily and disengage from your activity. Challenge yourself with goals that are easy to attain; this will boost your confidence, and gradually you can easily exceed these goals to attain new challenges. Setting goals will give you something to look forward to!
- *Keep your experience of exercising positive.* It's very important to keep yourself positive by encouraging and congratulating yourself once your exercise or activity is over. It's critical to change the way you psychologically perceive your exercise; again, let it be something that lifts you up and not something that burdens you. When you start an activity that you like, your body releases dopamine, popularly known as the pleasure molecule, to your brain. Dopamine

is a neurotransmitter, and the brain releases it when you do something that you desire, such as eating food that your crave, having sex, or doing any activity where a potential reward (pleasure) is anticipated. Dopamine contributes to a feeling of pleasure and gratification, hence boosting your mood and motivating you to keep repeating this act over and over again. Thus, making your exercise an enjoyable activity will send messages to your brain to receive it as a source of pleasure, therefore releasing dopamine. It's all about your mindset!

Go on a Healthy Diet

Studies have proven that going on a healthy diet can definitely improve mood and decrease the symptoms of anxiety. Anxiety is not a physical condition, but a reflection of thought. That's why a healthy diet manages the symptoms and not the roots of anxiety. A healthy diet consists of getting the right vitamins, enough minerals, and the essential nutrients. It's important to emphasize that in order for a healthy diet to help with your anxiety, you need to cut off caffeine products such as coffee, black tea, chocolate, weight loss pills, energy drinks, etc. Caffeine is a powerful stimulant that makes you nervous, so cutting it off will help you regulate your anxiety. Alcohol, like caffeine, is an anxiety stimulant, and it should be reduced as well. The perfect diet for anxiety is a diet that is high in plants and low in processed foods.

Foods Than Help Reduce Anxiety

- Low glycemic diet. This diet keeps your blood sugar level constant throughout the day. When you are anxious, or experience a panic attack, your body reacts as if it is experiencing low blood sugar levels. If your body sugar level wavers too much, then your body ends up releasing more adrenaline into your system, making you feel more at edge. Panic attacks can also be caused by a sudden drop in blood sugar levels, which makes you end up feeling more fearful and anxious. Foods that are recommended in a low glycemic diet are green

vegetables, fruits, carrots, chickpeas, kidney beans, lentils and all-bran cereals.
- Complex carbohydrates (aka comfort food). In her book *Potatoes Not Prozac*, Kathleen Desmaisons (1999) stresses the importance of incorporating healthy carbs into your diet. This, of course, does not mean artificial sweeteners, processed corn syrup, or starch, which are unhealthy for your body, but foods such as root vegetables and fruits are of high importance for fueling your body with energy and stabilizing your mood. Healthy carbs can be found in root vegetables, fruits (especially tropical fruits), legumes, nuts, and whole grains.
- Vitamins A, vitamins B6 and B12, and vitamins C, D and E. Deficiency in these vitamins plays a role in intensifying anxiety symptoms. Therefore, it is advised to go on a diet high in plants and low in processed foods. Plants that are rich in vitamins include dark leafy greens such as kale and spinach, seeds such as sunflower and flax, broccoli, mushrooms, nuts, avocadoes, sweet bell peppers, green peas, dried fruits, and tropical fruits.
- Magnesium. Magnesium greatly contributes to the creation of energy, formation of protein, and regulation of nerve cells. It is recommended that adult men take about 400 mg a day, while women should take around 310 mg. Magnesium-rich foods include pumpkin seeds,

almonds, spinach, cashews, peanuts, black beans, edamame, dark chocolate, whole wheats, potatoes, yogurt, kidney beans, bananas, milk, and organic salmon.

- Zinc. Studies show that zinc deficiency is associated with generalized anxiety, panic attacks, and even OCD. Thus, including zinc in your diet can help in boosting your immunity and mental health. An adequate intake of zinc for men is 11mg, while for women it is 8mg (*Office of Dietary Supplements - Zinc*, 2016). Various foods include zinc but oysters are richest in zinc; lobsters and crabs also have high levels. Other foods such as red meat and poultry provide sufficient amounts of zinc as well. Further food sources include nuts, beans, whole grains, and dairy products.
- Omega 3 or fish oil. Studies reveal that omega-3 has a positive impact on brain health, depression, and anxiety. Good food sources for omega-3 are fish, chia seeds, flax seeds, eggs, and walnuts (*Office of Dietary Supplements - Omega 3*, 2016).
- Water. Studies show that staying hydrated greatly influences your mental health. It is proven that dehydration causes brain function to slow down and also impedes the release of serotonin in the brain; thus, water is an essential nutrient for the brain.

Link Between An Unhealthy Diet and Anxiety Disorder

According to new Canadian research from the Canadian Longitudinal Study on Aging, those who have low intake of fruits and vegetables are at a risk of developing an anxiety disorder. People who "consume less than 3 sources of fruits and vegetables daily, presented at least at 24 percent higher odds of anxiety disorder diagnosis. This may also partly explain the findings associated with body composition measures. As levels of total body fat increased beyond 36 percent, the likelihood of anxiety disorder was increased by more than 70 percent. Increased body fat may be linked to greater inflammation. Emerging research suggests that some anxiety disorders can be linked to inflammation" (Read, 2020).

A poor diet can be a cause of health hazards, chronic pain, and illness. This plays a major role in developing anxiety disorders and elevating anxiety symptoms. Therefore, it is highly advised to consume foods that are rich in multivitamins, essential nutrients, and minerals to maintain good physical and mental health.

Chapter 3:

Stress Management

Stress can be hard to control, especially unidentified or unexpressed stress. Stress causes more blood to pump through your body, which may lead to high blood pressure, shortness in breath, panic, and anxiety. Studies show that 77% of our health problems are due to stress. Stress attacks the adrenal glands, which can trigger the body to flood with cortisol and adrenaline. During episodes of stress, adrenaline is released, and that increases your heart rate and blood pressure. Over time, this can cause health problems like high blood pressure, migraines, and/or digestion problems. Stress also affects your immunity; a study found that people who suffer from chronic stress are twice more likely to get a cold (Mayo Clinic Staff, 2019).

If left unresolved, stress may become chronic. That's why it's important to address your stress issues and find coping skills and strategies to overcome it like meditation, breathing techniques, and physical activities.

Signs of Stress

It may be possible that you are stressed but you do not know it. Your body gives you signals that alert you that it's time to destress:

- Appetite changes. Studies show that 88% of people who are stressed make unhealthy eating choices, whether they undereat or overeat. People who eat more when stressed choose unhealthy foods, such as sugary or greasy foods. (Read, 2020)
- Digestion issues. Stress can mess with your digestion; your brain and gut are controlled by many of the same hormones. A stressed brain can sometimes lead to heartburn, indigestion, nausea, vomiting, diarrhea, stomach pain, and/or bloating.
- Experience negative feelings. Acute and chronic stress are possible factors of depression. Stress causes you to feel tense, restless, or even depressed. Negative and dark thoughts will

hover in your mind, making you feel uneasy and anxious.
- Low energy and sleep issues. When feeling stressed, negative emotions and worries may keep you up at night, causing you a disrupted sleep or insomnia. In return, lack of sleep causes more stress.
- Deep breathing can become difficult. Stress and weary emotions can cause the breathing airway to constrict, resulting in shortness in breath and rapid breathing. Studies show that acute stress can even cause an asthma attack or a panic attack.
- Cravings for substance misuse become stronger. Consuming alcohol or drugs may give the brain immediate and temporary pleasure or relief; however, abusing substances can cause a lot of harm to your body.
- Skin problems. Stress causes skin breakouts and makes wounds heal more slowly.

Which Situations Make You Most Anxious?

Recognizing and acknowledging the sources of stress in your life is the first step in managing them. You may suffer from daily stressors such as having too much workload, failing a test, fighting with your partner, or not being able to achieve a certain goal. These are small or acute daily stressors that may not cause major problems or may not last for a long time. However, big stressors such as money or health problems, major life changes, loss of a loved one, or relationship conflicts may cause long-term or chronic stress, which can in turn cause further health problems.

Identify Your Personal Triggers

Stress may be caused by a range of personal and social issues such as traumatic events, relationship problems, or even health problems. The following are the common causes of stress; which ones do you identify with?

- Money. Having financial problems is the most common source of stress. Being in debt and the inability to provide for your family or yourself can add a significant amount of stress on you. This is something that almost everyone can relate to, since we live in a materialistic world where money is a major concern for everyone. Unemployment or the inability to find a suitable job is also another factor that contributes to adding stress.
- Work. Almost everyone you know suffers from job-related stressors. Whether you are a CEO or an intern, stress from work can sometimes be too overwhelming due to loaded responsibilities, unaccomplished jobs, due dates, and a negative work environment.

- Emotional problems. You may feel alone and misunderstood. Finding it hard to relate to someone can be overwhelming. Teenagers report that one of the main causes of stress in their lives is bullying or the inability to make friends. For many of us, not finding a partner and experiencing love can be stressful and even traumatic.
- Health issues. If you or a person close to you suffers from a chronic illness, or painful and discomforting symptoms of an illness, that can increase your stress. According to the American Psychological Association (APA), more than 50% of caregivers report feeling stressed by the amount of care they provide. Aging could be another cause of stress, for a person may feel sorry for lost opportunities, running out time, or fearing death. (*Depression and Caregiving | Family Caregiver Alliance*, 2020)
- Drastic life changes. Sweeping life changes such as the death of a loved one, breakup or divorce, changing jobs, and moving to a new house or country are examples of major life changes that can cause someone to feel tense and worried. Positive changes, such as retirement, moving to a new house, or getting married can also cause a serious amount of pressure and anxiety.
- Relationships. Conflicts with your partner, family member, or friend can add to your stress

levels. Divorce, separation, or loss can be major stress triggers that may cause a long-term effect.

- Traumatic events. People who have experienced traumatic events or life-threatening situations such as wars or natural disasters often live with long-term stress. Surviving a life-threatening experience would most probably cause a post-traumatic stress disorder (PTSD).
- Discrimination. A lot of people may not think of discrimination as a cause of stress, but feeling discriminated against can cause permanent or chronic stress. For instance, you may experience harassment at work due to your gender, race, or religious beliefs. This would definitely augment your worries, fears, and lack of confidence.
- Phobias. Living with constant and unwavering fear can be pretty exhausting and stressful.

Which of the above mentioned triggers can you identify with? Do you have any other specific triggers? If yes, write them down in the space below:

How to Manage Your Stress

Stress is our body's physical and biological response to any kind of demand, a mechanism that helps us survive. For instance, when encountering danger, such as a fire or a wild animal, our body instantly emits stress hormones that shut our vital functions in order to ready our body for fight or flight. Our brain turns off the prefrontal cortex, which is responsible for rational thought. When we feel the necessity to escape a physical danger, primal instincts become the most important. This mechanism is great to evade physical danger, but it's not so effective when it comes to daily emotional stressors, for we tend to suppress these fearful or worrisome emotions (which don't subject us to immediate danger). This leads to chronic stress, which affects us both physically and emotionally. According to studies, 75 to 90% of our health problems are stress related (George, 2017).

The World Health Organization (WHO) has identified stress as the "health epidemic of the 21st century." The stress we encounter today, especially at the workplace, is much more than the previous generations have experienced (George, 2017)

Here are some healthy tips for stress management:

- Remember, stress is our body's response to danger. When we experience any form of stress, our body expects a form of physical reaction. Therefore, when you experience acute emotional stress, take deep breaths which will strain and relax your muscles. This is a physical reaction (your body will think you're fighting back), and hence you will feel better.

- If you are feeling stressed due to a load of work or maybe feeling overwhelmed before a big test, take a few moments alone in a place where you feel safe, or maybe take a stroll out in nature. Spending time in nature improves energy levels, eases stress, and boosts your overall well-being. Again, this is a physical reaction that will help your body relax and release the negative emotions.
- If you get into a conflict with your spouse, family member, or even a colleague, it's a good idea to do any physical activity that requires a challenge, such as going for a karate session or punching a bag. This way, your body and brain will be tricked into thinking that you've accomplished a physical act of fighting back and beating up your opponent.
- Feeling stressed while doing your house chores? Dance! Put on some music and dance while you're cleaning. This way the task will be more enjoyable, and at the same time you exert physical effort to release your inner stress.
- Laugh! Laughing helps reduce anxiety and alleviates stress by stimulating your organs and decreasing your stress response. Laughing also lowers your heart rate and calms you down. If you can't find a reason to laugh, watch a comedy show!

- Connect with others, whether your friends or your pet. Talk to others and vent out your problems and worries. Don't forget to keep a smile on your face!
- Meditate. Meditation has proven to be an effective method in reducing stress while improving your sleep habits and cognitive function. If you don't know how to meditate, there are a lot of free online guided meditation videos.
- The most important tip is to manage the causes of your stress. Simplify your life and the problems around you. Disconnect with the materialistic things or your possessions. These are your possessions, so you possess and control them, and not the other way around. The more walls you build around yourself, the harder it'll be to break them down. Learn to manage your own internal system; focus on yourself and not the external stressors.

Here's a chart that will aid you to follow up with your heart rate as well as your emotional state. Keep track of how you feel over a period of seven days, and you will notice a change in your physical and emotional state.

Physical Activity	Heart Rate Before	Heart Rate After	Emotional State

Put an End to Chronic Nervousness and Uneasiness

Anxiety doesn't always make sense. Most of the time, you feel anxious without really knowing what is behind the feeling. You feel edgy but you really can't comprehend why. That's why it is necessary to understand why you are anxious, acknowledge and experience this anxiety, and then tackle it. You shouldn't aim to completely eliminate anxiety, because there will always be triggers, but once you accept and confront your worries and fears, it'll be easier to control and manage them.

Acknowledge, Confront, and Reflect on Your Fears

You can't get rid of anxiety by simply getting rid of it. In fact, you can't really get rid of anxiety completely, but you can fight it. First, you have to acknowledge it.

Fighting means confronting and not avoiding a problem. Don't dodge social or anxious situations by retreating to your safe zone or running away to avoid the possible horrible emotions that you may feel.

Anxiety is the place where fear resides, so you have to be curious and start noticing where your fear is derived from. Most of our fears come from our childhood years or traumatic incidents. Many of our fears are unreasonable and shaped when we are children; however, they frequently reappear in our adult lives, where they transform into overreactions. Next time you feel anxious, try to pinpoint why you're restless or fearful. Ask yourself questions like, what triggered this feeling? Was it something someone said? Was it something you've experienced that brought back an unhappy memory?

It may happen to be that you're having a normal day when suddenly something makes you shudder or stand still. You'd feel hot and blush and get the sudden urge to flee. This is what some scholars call "hot cognition," a mental process by which emotions influence your reasoning and decision making. When your body and your brain react to a certain stimulus that makes you anxious, you need to dig deep to figure out the main trigger of your emotions. This is the first step of battling your anxiety.

Hot cognition drives you towards an irrational response, but this is only normal. This is where the neuropsychology of fear is at play, and this is what is known as fight or flight reaction. You experience increased heart rate and blood pressure, rapid breathing, and your pupils might dilate. Your pituitary gland releases 30 stress hormones into your bloodstream. This is your body's readiness for energy production, a mechanism to help you survive sudden and dangerous situations.

When your body starts reacting to a stressful event, try to be aware of it and not immediately react. You don't have to run away, shout, or even text anyone. Instead, reflect on what you are feeling. A good way to do so is to keep a record or an anxiety diary. The best way to tackle fear is to acknowledge it, look it in the eye, and recognize the impact it has on your life. The more you can identify panic responses, the better you can win over them.

Our natural and innate response of fight-or-flight dominates the right responses, causing us to run and hide. An alternative to that is confrontation.

Confrontation is a form of exposure therapy, where fear gradually is normalized and its effect becomes less.

Repetitive and most importantly gradual and gentle exposure to the source of your specific worry or phobia and the thoughts, feelings, and sensations related to it will aid you to control your anxiety.

Let's say you have terrible stage fright, but you have a great opportunity to give a speech that would be great for your career. The first step you need to take is to acknowledge your cause of fear, which is public speaking. Then, you have to acknowledge the impact of this fear on your life and decisions. Would it be worth fighting against? Next, evaluate the risks that you may encounter and the possibilities of these risks. Educate yourself about facts and risks of being the center of public attention and decide whether your fear is rational or not. Remember, you have to take baby steps! Start gently and gradually to put yourself in a similar situation that would make you feel frightful. You can maybe start with a mindful experience of what it's like for you to be on stage, how you'd feel, and what you would do to alleviate your worries. The next step is to prepare your speech in front of a mirror or even videotape yourself. That way, you can reflect on your errors and work on them. Give your speech a try in front of a small audience that you feel comfortable with, and ask them for feedback. When you are ready to finally get on stage, you will still feel scared, but you have to embrace this feeling and not focus on it. Take deep breaths and trust yourself. You may stutter, blush, and your hands may become sweaty, but keep telling yourself that you can do it, you can overcome it, you can beat it.

Can you identify your fears? Whether you have one or more, list them in the space below:

Guided Self-Meditation to Ease Your Worries and Fears

Guided meditation is also known as guided imagery or visualization. In this technique of meditation you use as many senses as possible, such as sights, smells, sounds, and even textures to form mental images of places or situations that you find relaxing. This is usually accompanied by a guide or a teacher.

Don't worry whether you're practicing the 'right' meditation or not, for it will only add up to your stress. You may refer to a professional instructor, or follow along with an audio or video and listen attentively to the trainer. But if you feel that you can do this on your own, go ahead.

Meditating doesn't have to be formal or complicated. All that is actually required is a few minutes of quality time alone with yourself.

First, you need to choose a quiet setting where you won't be interrupted by any distractions. Find a comfortable position, whether sitting or lying down, and try to be as comfortable as you can be while keeping a good posture during your meditation. Turn off your cell phone, radio, or any other source of disturbance. Next, focus your attention on a specific object, image, mantra, or of course on your breathing. Shut off your thoughts completely, and be aware to keep on silencing your thoughts whenever they come up again while letting calming thoughts come to your mind without any judgment. Breathing is the main technique of meditation. It involves deep and evenly paced breathing in which you use your diaphragm muscle to expand your lungs. You can use a counting method. Start by taking a slow deep breath and feeling the air fill up to the bottom of your lungs, then pause for five seconds and exhale for 10 seconds as you completely empty your lungs. Repeat this technique four to five times until you find yourself totally relaxed.

Once you find yourself calmer, visualize a setting that you like. It could be a beach, a lake, or any other natural scene. Try to envision the details in this setting: the trees, hills, water color, water temperature, and the scents around you. Allow your senses to imagine these sensations and enjoy them. Imagine yourself standing in this setting, head up, facing the sun, allowing a soft breeze to caress your face and skin. Imagine you have a backpack on your shoulders, heavy with all the life burdens that you put on your shoulders. Keep on breathing at your own comfortable pace until you decide to let go of this backpack. Drop it and let your shoulders feel the weight lifted off them. You can also imagine yourself floating on water, feeling the cool water surrounding your body in total relaxation. In this type of meditation, you can concentrate on a sacred image, person, or setting, integrating feelings of love, empathy, and gratefulness into your contemplations.

Once you try this guided self-medication, reflect on this experience in the space below. Was it easy to dodge your thoughts? Were you able to follow the breathing strategy? How did you feel after?

Chapter 4:

Relaxing Techniques

There are several relaxing techniques that you can practice in order to calm your anxiety and take control of your emotions. Doctors highly recommend breathing techniques as an immediate resort to alleviate the symptoms of anxiety or panic. Meditation and mindfulness are methods that you can incorporate in your lifestyle, which have proven to be very effective in organizing thoughts, managing stress, and letting go of negative energy.

Breathing Techniques

Breathing techniques are essential to calming anxiety as they expand the diaphragm, strengthen the lungs, and relieve your stress. If it's the first time you've tried any breathing technique, you may feel a bit dizzy or like you're about to pass out, but don't worry. Practice according to your own pace and always listen to your body.

Different Breathing Exercises to Try

- Box or square breathing technique. This method helps relieve stress and anxiety, and it is especially used by the military for special ops missions as they help relax soldiers before they go in battle. This technique pretty much resembles its name as it is divided into four simple steps. First, you inhale for four seconds, then hold your breath for another four seconds, exhale for four seconds, and finally hold your breath again for four seconds. You can also use imagery or visualization as you practice this technique, by focusing your attention on a single object or image. You can use your finger moving it along with the square as you breathe in, hold your breath, breathe out, and hold your breath again. Repeat this process four to five times.

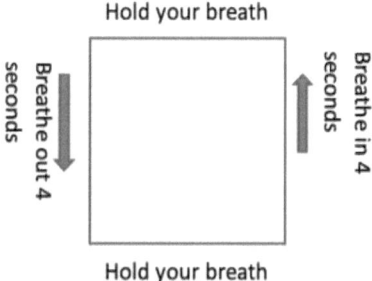

- Pursed lips. This technique involves belly breathing, or diaphragmatic breathing. That means breathing in through your belly instead of through your chest; you can put your hands on your belly and feel your breath going in. First, you breathe in for four seconds, then purse your lips and breathe out for eight seconds. Repeat four to five times until you're feeling relaxed.

- Focused breathing. Breathing deeply and slowly in a focused manner can help ease anxiety. You can practice this technique by sitting or lying down in a silent, relaxing place. First, pay attention to how it feels when you inhale and exhale naturally. As you do so, scan your body mentally. As you inhale, visualize the inhaled air washing over your body, and as you exhale, visualize all the negative and toxic energy exiting your body. You may sense tension in parts of your body that you never noticed before. As you breathe slowly through your nose, place your hand on your belly and notice how your belly and upper body are expanding. When you exhale, do it naturally, or in the form of a sigh. Keep doing so for a few minutes, while concentrating on the rise and fall of your chest and abdomen. It's a good idea to pick a word to focus on (such as 'safe,' 'calm,' or 'free') and vocalize during your exhale. When you get distracted, smoothly return your attention to your breathing and your words. Keep doing this technique for around 20 minutes daily for effective results.

- Alternate nostril breathing. To practice this technique, start by sitting in a quiet and comfortable place, stretching your spine, relaxing your shoulders, and opening your chest. Place your left hand on your knee, raise your right hand, and put the pointer and middle fingers of your right hand on your forehead in between the eyebrows. Breathe in and out through your nose, while having your eyes closed. Then, close the right-side nostril using your right thumb and inhale slow and deeply through your left-side nostril. Hold your breath for two to three seconds and then repeat the procedure on your left-side nostril. Practice this set of inhaling and exhaling across each nostril for 10 times.

- Lion's breath. This technique is about forceful exhaling. To practice lion's breath, you should sit in a kneeling position, crossing your ankles and lying your bottom on your feet. You can also sit cross legged if you find the first kneeling position is uncomfortable. Next, stretch out your arms and fingers, and place your hands to your knees. Start by inhaling through your nose and exhaling through your mouth, vocalizing a 'ha' sound. As you breathe out, open your mouth as wide as you can and stretch out your tongue. Bring your focus (while exhale) on your forehead (third eye) or your nose. As you inhale again, relax your face. You can repeat this practice five to six times.

How Breathing Can Help Your Body Relax

Having tried the different breathing techniques, which one do you find best? Have you noticed how breathing can make you feel relaxed? The next time you try any breathing technique, reflect on how your body feels. Mindful breathing practices can help you relax due to the fact that they cause your body to feel the way it does when you are calm and stress-free.

Deep breathing (diaphragmatic breathing) allows more oxygen to flow into your body to aid in calming your nerves, alleviating stress and anxiety. It is a vital method to relieve the body from stress since when you take a deep breath, a message is sent to your nervous system to ease the tension and calm down. The brain in turn sends this message to your body to reduce the symptoms of stress of panic, such as increased heart rate, rapid breathing, pain levels, and/or high blood pressure.

Breathing techniques are effective and easy to do on your own and at any setting. You can choose which ones work best for you; though it may take practice, they are instantly beneficial.

This is because of how your nervous system functions. Your nervous system is autonomic, which means it panels involuntary actions like the heart rate. The nervous system is made of two parts that work alternately (if one is activated, the other repressed): the sympathetic nervous system and the parasympathetic nervous system. The first controls our fight-or-flight responses, while the latter controls our relaxation response.

When you breathe deeply, more carbon dioxide enters your blood, which mollifies sections of the brain (such as the amygdala) that handle your anxiety response by synchronizing your heart rate and breathing.

Practicing Mindfulness

What is Mindfulness? How Can It Help Reduce Anxiety?

Many people have the misconception that mindfulness is complicated and can't be practiced by just anyone. In fact, mindfulness is pretty easy and far from complicated. This term has been widely spread in the past few years because a lot of people have been learning more about the numerous positive impacts it has proven to have on the mind and body. Mindfulness does not only help to reduce stress and anxiety, but it also teaches you to like yourself and your life more every day.

You may wonder, is mindfulness a practice or a way of living? It is both. You practice mindfulness, and gradually it becomes a part of life as you become more mindful in your everyday life.

Mindfulness is defined by Merriam-Webster dictionary as "the practice of maintaining a non-judgmental state of heightened or complete awareness of one's thoughts, emotions, or experiences on a moment-to-moment basis." Simply put, it means the state of being present, being aware of the moment, and reflecting on what is in and around us. Most of our anxieties come due to our constant worrying about the future or reminiscing about painful memories. Of course, it's not all negative; we may be excited about events in the future or remember happy memories, but how often do we spend time focusing on the moment and deliberately living the present? Mindfulness allows us to detach ourselves from our thoughts and emotions without identifying them as positive or negative.

Through focusing on the present moment, mindfulness thwarts remembering and worrying. Excessive worrying about the future and constantly remembering the painful past can make us pretty anxious. That's why mindfulness can be an effective tool to bring our attention to the present moment. Research has proven that mindfulness helps with overcoming depression and anxiety. It teaches us how to react to stress while being aware of what's happening in and around us in the present moment, rather than responding impulsively while being unmindful of what feelings or reasons are there. As we learn how to be aware of our physical and mental state in the moment, we acquire more adaptive responses to challenging situations (Kind, 2014)

Mindfulness also helps us understand and accept our emotions. Therefore, we become better at recognizing, experiencing, and managing our emotions. We become more open-minded and perceive things from different viewpoints. For instance, if your boss snaps at you, you might feel guilty and worry that you've done something horrible. If you try to detach yourself from your immediate response, which is being harmed, you might realize that your boss has been overwhelmed by work himself and just released his anger at you. Seeing things from a different perspective can lighten some of your worry and negative emotions.

The following are the benefits of practicing mindfulness:

- **Body awareness:** When you practice mindfulness, you'll be able to recognize sensations in your body and thus become more aware of your body. When you are mindful of your internal emotions, you will be able to control and better understand these emotions.
- **Physical health:** There are also health benefits for practicing mindfulness, such as decreased blood pressure as well as cholesterol.
- **Mental health:** Many psychotherapists turn to mindfulness meditation to treat many mental

illnesses, such as depression, anxiety, obsessive-compulsive disorder, addiction, and eating disorders.

- **Self-awareness:** As mentioned earlier, mindfulness makes you like yourself and your life more, since it helps you perceive yourself in a better way. Studies have shown that mindfulness boots self-acceptance and confidence (Kind, 2014).
- **Focused attention:** As mindful practice improves your ability to focus, it also helps in improving your attention abilities. This will help you bring your full attention when needed at a certain task, instead of being distracted with worry.
- **Sound Sleep**: Studies have shown that mindfulness meditation can aid in having a sound night's sleep. The study mentions that mindfulness tends to "increase the relaxation response through its function of increasing attentional factors that impart control over the autonomic nervous system" (Black et al., 2015).
- **Overall well-being:** Being more mindful encourages many positive approaches to a contented life. You become more receptive to pleasure and more enthusiastic to engage in physical and social activities. When you focus your entire attention in the present moment, you will be less anxious about the future or past regrets, more inspired towards building your

self-esteem, and better at forming profound relations with others around you. Studies have also shown that mindfulness practice can enhance women's sex life by silencing any mental rants that cross their minds and block the pleasure of the sexual act (Kind, 2014).

How to Practice Mindfulness

Here's a simple eight-step mindfulness practice:

1—Search for a quiet and comfortable place and dedicate a time for yourself. Find a tranquil place in the house and use it only for meditation. This way, whenever you sit in this place, your body will be notified that it is time to relax and meditate. Make sure there aren't any distractions around, so put your phone on silent mode and turn off all electronics.

2—Sit down in any position you find comfortable. Close your eyes and breathe naturally. Focus on your thoughts and silence them one by one. Don't think about the future or the past, and place your full attention on the present. Accept yourself fully and link yourself with the present moment. Whenever you feel yourself getting distracted, focus again on your breathing and the sounds around you. Acknowledge anything that comes at the moments, whether they are sounds, smells, or emotions.

3—Consider this time that you are spending a mindful time for your body to recharge so you can be productive and effective in whatever you have to do after. Allow yourself to be conscious of the moment, appreciating this resting period for yourself, and consider it an essential aspect of leading a contented life.

4—Detach yourself completely from the past and the future. Whatever happened to your past is done and can't be changed. Even if the worst happened, so what? This is the question you should ask yourself when you think of your past, no matter how painful it was. So what? As for the future, well, it's not here yet and any kind of intense worry is irrational. What matters is the now, the present. This is where you are and this is where your focus should be. Stop thinking about the concept of time and forget about the watch.

5—Consider your thoughts, actions, and behavior. What is the purpose behind your actions? When you say something, or tell someone anything, ask yourself, how would it benefit you and them? Consider the purpose and the reason behind your words and your feelings and ask yourself, is it worth it? Don't allow your thoughts to hold negative or bad intentions; be determined to let goodness into your life. Acknowledge your judgments and let them pass along with your thoughts. These judgments may not last long, because the mind can always change.

6—Make sure that no matter where your mind drifts, you always bring it back to the present moment. Be conscious again that the past is behind you and there's nothing you can do to alter it, and now is not the time to worry about the future. Come back to the present moment where there is peace and tranquility.

7—Our mind works in a stream of thoughts, so it's only natural if you find yourself again drifting away. Acknowledge the present thought and let it pass. Take a few deep breaths and bring your attention back to your mindfulness practice.

8—You can always add some tranquil and relaxing music to your mindfulness practice. Choose any kind of meditation or spa music and focus on the sounds that you hear.

Once you try this mindful meditation, reflect on this experience in the space below. Was it easy to dodge your thoughts? Were you able to follow the breathing strategy? How did you feel after?

Meditation

Mindfulness and meditation are not the same. Mindfulness is being aware of the present while focusing on thoughts, feelings, behavior, and everything else. While mindfulness is being aware of the present, meditation is full detachment from everything. Mindfulness can be practiced at any time or place, while meditation is practiced for a specific duration. Though they are different, they are like mirror reflections of each other. Mindfulness stimulates and leads the way to meditation, while meditation fosters and magnifies mindfulness.

How Meditation Helps in Reducing Anxiety

Meditation can benefit both the body and mind. It provides a feeling of tranquility, peace, and balance for a period that extends beyond your meditation time. When you meditate, you're allowing positive energy and peaceful emotions to conquer your body and mind. This helps you to get rid of negative thoughts, overwhelming emotions, or built-up stress and tension.

Meditation fortifies your emotional well-being and provides you with the following benefits:

- Acquiring abilities to manage and control your stress
- Increasing your self-awareness, self-love, and confidence
- Detachment from negative thoughts that make you anxious
- Gradually letting go of negative emotions
- Perceiving new stressful situations in a different perspective
- Stretching your imagination and growing your creativity
- Fostering patience and tolerance
- Improving sleep
- Alleviating anxiety and depression symptoms
- Easing your physical pains, even if they are chronic

Types of Meditation to Practice

Meditation comes in different forms and types, but all have the same goal in common: accomplishing internal peace.

There following are types of meditation that you can try:

- **Guided meditation**: As explained earlier, guided meditation is a form of meditation in which you visualize a peaceful setting while connecting with your senses.
- **Mindfulness meditation**: As mentioned earlier, mindfulness and meditation are linked. Mindful meditation is a practice in which you practice being mindful, or having the ability to bring your complete focus to the present moment. In this kind of meditation, you expand your conscious awareness as you focus on your breathing. You notice and acknowledge your thoughts and feelings and allow them to pass without any judgment.
- **Yoga**: This is the most popular form of meditation in which you exercise different postures and breathing techniques to boost your body's flexibility and mind's peace. Yoga trains your body and mind as the different postures involve physical balance and focus on the present time.
- **Mantra meditation**: This form of meditation requires a silent repeat of a calming word such as 'om,' a calming thought, or a prayer. The repeating of the calming sounds helps you block out all your thoughts and focus on your mantra.
- **Tai chi**: If you like to add physical activity to your meditation, then this is the right type of

meditation for you. Tai chi is a kind of soothing Chinese martial art, in which you practice a chain of positions or movements in a gentle, slow way while breathing deeply.

- **Transcendental Meditation**: This is a spiritual type of meditation and amplified mindfulness, in which you sit still, breathing slowly and calmly, aiming to transcend or go beyond your current state. Focusing on a mantra is also included in transcendental meditation, and it can be done with a practitioner or a group. The mantra to be chosen has to be something that reflects motivation and positivity, such as repeating the phrase "I'm strong."

- **Chakra Meditation**: This is a type of meditation that aims to unblock the seven chakras. With appropriate chakra meditation, you will be able to purify and balance your chakras to maintain your spiritual, emotional and physical wellbeing, as well as a peaceful state of mind.

The seven chakras are as follows:
1. Root Chakra (Muladhara): This chakra's color is red and its mantra is 'LAM.' The root chakra is situated at the very bottom of your spine and connects you to the wider world and your essential needs for food, protection, and stability.
2. Sacral Chakra (Svadhisthana): This chakra's color is orange and its mantra is 'VAM.' The sacral chakra is found below the belly button. It reigns both your reproductive organs and your creativity.
3. Solar Plexus Chakra (Manipura): This chakra's color is yellow and its mantra is 'RAM.' The solar plexus chakra is found in your stomach. This chakra manages

digestion, as well as your mental and spiritual being.

4. Heart Chakra (Anahata): This chakra's color is green and its mantra is 'YAM.' The heart chakra is found at the center of your heart and is connected to your heart and lungs. Thus, it manages the respiratory system, blood flow, and emotional connections to others.
5. Throat Chakra (Visshuddha): This chakra's color is blue and its mantra is 'HAM.' Just like its name, the throat chakra is found in the throat, next to your thyroid. This chakra when balanced, enhances communication and self-expression. It also manages hormones.
6. Third Eye Chakra (Ajna): This chakra's color is indigo and its mantra is 'SHAM.' The third eye chakra is located right over the joint of the eyebrows. It is responsible for perception and intuition.
7. Crown Chakra (Sahasrara): This chakra's color is purple or white, and its mantra is 'OM.' The crown chakra is the most powerful chakra; it rests on the top of the head. Once your chakras are balanced, the crown chakra acts as a supreme connection to the broader

world and maintains a feeling of tranquility, strength, and stability.

Links to Guided Meditation and Meditation Music

You don't need to waste time and money on going to a meditation training, unless you feel like joining a meditation group or getting a professional to help you meditate. There are numerous videos online that can guide you on the steps to meditate, or offer your meditative music to listen to as you meditate alone. Here are some links that you can start with:

- Back To Basics Guided Meditation
- Mindfulness Meditation
- Yoga For Anxiety and Stress
- Guided Meditation Using a Mantra to Set Your Intentions
- Om Mantra Meditation
- Tai Chi 5 Minutes a Day
- Guided Meditation for Transcendence
- Open Balance Chakras, Heal & Sleep
- Quick 7 Chakra Cleansing
- Peaceful Meditation Music, Deep Relaxing & Healing Music
- Let go of Anxiety, Fear & Worries: A Guided Meditation
- 15 Minute Super Deep Meditation Music

Chapter 5:

Anxiety Relapses

You may fear that once you've made the right changes in your life and managed to overcome your anxiety, one day you may relapse and lose all the hard work that you've accomplished. This is very normal, and many people share the same feeling. When you do all the right practices and follow a healthy lifestyle, you incorporate these positive changes into your life, but many go through certain lapses due to going back to old bad habits. A lapse does not mean that you're relapsing, but multiple and continuous lapses may lead to a relapse.

Difference Between a Lapse and a Relapse

There's an obvious difference between a lapse and a relapse. A lapse is a short return to old bad habits; this is completely normal, especially if the lapse is triggered by accumulated stress or simply having a bad day. A relapse, on the other hand, is a complete return to an old unhealthy lifestyle, along with the bad habits that used to cause anxiety. When someone relapses, he or she goes back to doing the same things that they did before starting the new positive changes.

For example, let's say you have low tolerance for alcohol and whenever you used to drink, the feeling of drunkenness or hangover made you panic. You work on your drinking habits and acknowledge that it is a trigger that you need to eliminate from your life. After going a few months alcohol free, you experience a painful event and you end up having a couple of drinks at the end of the day. This could be considered a lapse, for you've returned to a bad habit once due to a certain trigger. However, if the drinking continues on a daily basis, going back to excessive drinking and the feeling of the horrible hangovers, then you've probably relapsed because you've lost control over the bad habits.

How you deal with a lapse determines whether it'll turn into a relapse or not. After having a lapse, your attitude towards it should be positive. If you consider your lapse a failure or a disappointment, then you will most probably give up on the healing process and slowly find yourself relapsing. However, if you consider your lapse a simple slip-up that you can recover from, then you will be heading towards avoiding a relapse.

How to Avoid a Relapse

The first step to avoid a relapse is acceptance. If you lapse, accept this slip-up and take control of the situation. If you experience panic or anxiety during your lapse, apply the breathing and meditation practices mentioned earlier. Set your mind to be determined not to slip again and identify what triggered your lapse. Here are some tips to help you avoid having a lapse and/or a relapse:

1—Don't give up. A lapse does not mean that you've failed and you should go hard on yourself. Motivate yourself to maintain your good and healthy habits and don't allow yourself to lose control over your behaviors and thoughts.

2—Think of your mental health as similar as your physical health. To maintain physical health, you eat healthy, exercise, get enough sleep, and keep a positive mindset. The same goes with your mental health; it needs maintenance and constant motivation to keep it going the right way.

3—Keep on practicing. Your perseverance in practicing the skills learned in this book is the ultimate way to prevent a lapse. Keep training yourself on being mindful, meditate daily, exercise regularly, and stick to your healthy diet. Practice makes perfect. If you feel you're not proficient yet at meditation and mindfulness, keep practicing and you will get there.

4—Identify the warning signs. When you have a lapse, make sure to notice what caused it. Be conscious of what makes you vulnerable and make a list of warning signs that indicate that your anxiety might be growing more intense. The list could include the following:

- Too much workload
- Unhappy relationship

- Major life change (getting married, moving to a new place, childbirth, loss of a loved one, etc.)
- Multiplied responsibilities at work or home
- Unhappy or dark thoughts

5—Prepare an action plan. When you recognize your warning signs, you can prepare a plan for how to manage them. Your plan may include:

- Taking some time off from work
- Spending some quality time alone to meditate
- Practicing mindfulness and breathing techniques
- Resting while doing something that you enjoy such as reading

6—Keep on challenging yourself. You are a work in progress, and there's always a room for improvement. A good way to avoid a lapse is to think of other changes that need to be done in your life. Are there any other fears that you need to confront and overcome? Is there any other bad habit that you need to break? Give yourself new challenges which will focus your attention on something new and distract you from the trigger that might cause you a lapse.

7—Reflect on your previous lapses and learn from them. Reflecting on any slip-up or mistake is very beneficial. This helps you evaluate the situation and recognize what triggered your lapse in the first place. Reflecting on the intensity of your anxiety or panic and the way you cope with it will help you pinpoint your strong and weak points. How intense was it? Was it bearable? Did it take you by surprise? How were you able to cope with it? What can you do better the next time? It's a good idea to keep a journal and jot down your reflections; this will help you take control of the next stressful situation.

8—It's impossible to go back to square one. You may go hard on yourself and consider yourself a failure if you lapse, thinking that you've undone all the hard work and progress, but this is so not true. You can never 'unlearn' a skill! Once you acquire the skills of breathing, mindfulness, and controlling your thoughts and emotions, there's no way that you go back to the time when you first started. Even if you relapse, be sure that you can always get yourself back on track. It's all about your mindset. It may have taken you months to be able to cope with your anxiety, but if you relapse, it won't take you as much. You just need to go back to practicing the right habits and performing the right techniques, and soon you'll find yourself getting a grip of your situation.

9—Don't be too hard on yourself. You're not perfect, and just like everyone else, you are susceptible to making mistakes. Go easy on yourself and remind yourself that lapses are normal. It's your attitude towards the lapse that matters. You can even consider a lapse a blessing in disguise, for it will only teach you how to deal with the next time and will give you more control over your anxiety. Be kind to yourself, acknowledge your mistakes, deal with them, and move forward.

10—Reward yourself. Just like you praise others for their good work, give yourself a pat on the back when you see yourself progressing and overcoming challenges. A reward may be going on a getaway, buying yourself something that you'd enjoy, or even pampering yourself with a spa! Coping with anxiety is a long process and surely deserves to be rewarded.

If you have lapsed or relapsed, reflect on the reasons and consequences in the space below.

Why did you lapse?	
Did you go back to any of your previous bad habits? Which ones?	
How did it feel?	
Why shouldn't you let yourself lapse again?	

Breaking Bad Habits

Coping with anxiety and acquiring good habits is a lifestyle. These habits can be considered coping mechanisms, but not all coping mechanisms are the same. For instance, playing a video game to distract yourself from what's triggering your anxiety is only a temporary solution, but once you finish playing your video game, you will realize that your anxiety isn't fully healed or may return very soon. That's why there are specific practices that will help you in the long run.

There are habits that you go to in order to avoid the anxiety symptoms, but these habits can actually be bad for you. The following are some examples of bad habits that may lead you to relapse:

1. Isolation: A lot of time you may find yourself not in the mood to socialize with others, and instead decide to be alone. You would spend the whole day scrolling on your phone or watching movies. While this may be a convenient way to relax, it could also be dangerous, for gradually it becomes your comfort zone and you will find it hard to get out of it. Whenever you feel yourself getting lazy and not in the mood to be active, allow yourself an hour or two to relax, but don't let it extend more than that. Force yourself out of it and do something that requires a certain activity, preferably outdoors.

2. Canceling Plans: We all cancel plans when we are not feeling too well, but making it a habit to cancel plans and ignore social occasions is a sign that you may be relapsing. Your friends and family might notice this, and consider it as a warning sign to commit to these plans and setting your mind that you should go on with the plans and that you will enjoy them.

3. Procrastination: You often procrastinate when you feel overwhelmed, but you don't realize that it can turn into a habit. This overwhelmed feeling can get your mind to rush with irrational and dark thoughts. It would be beneficial to make a to-d0 list in which you prioritize and break your chores or work into chunks. This way it'll be easy to get things done without getting anxious. Set your mind into believing that you want to be productive, and start with the most important tasks. Soon you'll find yourself slipping out of your anxiety.

4. Anger Bursts: Do you ever find yourself lashing out at people around for the most trivial reasons? Do you find yourself saying horrible things to others that you regret later? Do you find yourself irritated by the simplest things such as noises? Do you feel that you can't control everything around you and it gets you more anxious and irritable? These are signs that your anxiety is getting out of control and you need to take control and manage your thoughts, emotions, and behavior. Whenever you find yourself in such a situation, go to your meditation place, take 10 to 15 minutes, and practice mindfulness meditation. Shut out your thoughts and focus on the moment, or visualize your happy place where you are in full control. Scan your body and relax every muscle of your body; this will help you recharge and let go of the negative emotions.

5. Shutting Down: This usually happens when you are overwhelmed with everyday problems and you feel that you cannot deal with them anymore. You become anxious just by thinking of them, so you decide to shut everything down. Also, this can happen when you get into an argument or a fight with your spouse or a family member. You may tend to internalize your thoughts and emotions and not speak up. Suppressing thoughts and emotions is not a way to deal with things. You are shutting yourself from what is external, thus causing yourself to get more anxious. You should learn to open up to others and not fear expressing yourself. You may also meditate to set your thoughts straight before you approach others and open up to them.

6. Smoking and Alcohol Drinking: While smoking a cigarette and having a drink may ease anxiety symptoms momentarily, in the long term they can make your anxiety even worse. A lot of people tend to turn to alcohol and smoking when having a lapse, but the ultimate thing is to be aware of it happening briefly and not turning again into a habit, and hence, a relapse.

7. Overeating: While many people refrain from eating while feeling anxious or depressed, many others tend to overeat. Overeating due to anxiety tends to be very unhealthy for you as you will most probably binge on junk and unhealthy foods. A good idea would be not purchasing any junk food and keeping it at your house. If you feel hungry, munch on healthy snacks only and don't allow yourself to spree on harmful foods.

Chart to Identify Bad Habits and Ways to Overcome Them

Bad Habit	What do you get out of it?	How does it impact you?	What can it be replaced with?	How would it help if you removed this trigger?

Chapter 6:

Therapy and Medication

Self-help and leading a healthy lifestyle has proven to be effective in dealing with anxiety. However, a lot of people prefer to resort to medication and psychotherapy in order to overcome their anxieties. It's not a simple process to find the right medication or treatment because each body responds differently than the other. Hence, if one treatment does show to be effective, try including another simultaneously. Research exhibits that psychotherapy can be beneficial even for people who do not react appropriately to medications. For anxiety disorders, cognitive-behavioral therapy (CBT), antidepressants, and anti-anxiety medications have been proven to be effective. Research largely indicates that psychotherapy is much more helpful than medications, and using medications along with therapy does not drastically enhance the outcomes. Both psychotherapy and medications require commitment, for the outcomes usually take a few weeks to be noticed. Thus, if you are planning to start a treatment, you should be completely willing to stick to it. Discussing the method of treatment with your doctor is highly recommended. You should understand it perfectly so it will make sense to you, so don't be hesitant in asking your doctor all the necessary questions concerning your condition.

When to Seek Professional Help?

When anxiety starts to interfere with your daily life, relationships, work, or physical health, then it's time for you to seek professional help. Here are some warning signs that indicate that you should consult with your doctor:

- You isolate yourself and don't speak up.
- Your chronic worry interrupts your life, whether at work, home, or your relationships.
- Your anxiety causes you to feel exhausted and easily fatigued.
- Your fears and worries stop you from accomplishing your work.
- Your fears or phobias stand in the way of accomplishing important tasks.
- You experience panic attacks regularly.
- Anxiety is consistent and lasts more than a few weeks.
- Your anxiety affects your physical health.
- You face problems in your relationships due to your anger bursts or irritation.
- Your anxiety becomes too much to handle alone.

Therapy

Therapy is the most effective option to battle anxiety. Unlike medication, therapy treats more than just the symptoms of anxiety, but it can help you uncover the underlying causes of it. Through therapy, you can learn how to relax; view situations in a new, less frightening perspective; and develop better coping mechanisms and problem-solving skills. Therapy provides you with the tools to defeat anxiety, and in the process, you learn how to use these tools in order for them to become a part of your life. The typical treatment for anxiety includes psychological counseling and therapy.

There are two leading approaches of therapy to treat anxiety:

Cognitive Behavioral Therapy (CBT)

Cognitive behavioral therapy is the most popular therapy for anxiety disorders. Studies have revealed it to be successful in the treatment of many anxiety disorders, such as generalized anxiety, social anxiety, panic, phobias, obsessive compulsive disorder, and others. This kind of therapy tackles negative patterns of thoughts and the misconceptions in the way we perceive the world and ourselves. It is evidently comprised of two aspects:

- Cognitive therapy, which assesses how negative cognitions (thoughts) trigger anxiety.

- Behavioral therapy, which assesses behaviors and reactions in conditions that prompt anxiety.

CBT emphasizes that our cognition (not our surroundings) influences our feelings. That is, our feelings are not generated by the situation we're in, but by how we perceive the situation. Consider the following example and the three different thoughts that could come to your mind and how these thoughts would affect how you feel, hence your decision.

Situation: You've been invited to a gala dinner		
First thought	*Dressing up and attending a gala dinner is thrilling. It'll be wonderful to meet new people!*	Feelings: Excited, joyful
Second thought	*I don't care about such formal events. They're boring. I'd rather stay home and binge on Netflix.*	Feelings: Indifferent, neutral
Third thought	*I don't have anything to wear. It'll be awkward and I will surely embarrass myself.*	Feelings: Anxious, negative

	I'm so not in the mood to meet anyone new.	

You can notice that the same event can stimulate three different emotional reactions. It all depends on your expectations and attitude. Negative thoughts generate negative emotions, such as fear and anxiety, while positive thoughts create excitement and happiness.

The emphasis of cognitive behavioral therapy for anxiety is first to identify the negative thoughts, and second to amend these thoughts that trigger negative emotions. What you think is what you feel; therefore, you should change the way you think, making it more positive and optimistic.

CBT depends on cognitive restructuring, or thought challenging, which is a method in which you learn to challenge the negative and irrational thoughts that affect your anxiety and substitute them with positive and realistic thoughts. This process follows three simple steps:

- First step: Detect negative and irrational thoughts. People with anxiety tend to have exaggerated reactions to certain situations. For example, if you have hydrophobia, you'd probably panic just by approaching a children's pool, and would see being in water as life-threatening. You may easily recognize that your fear is irrational, but it's not that easy to identify your irrational, scary thoughts. That's why you have to challenge yourself and try to comprehend why you thought that way, what were the risks, and what images came to your mind. Of course, this step will be done with the help of your therapist.

- Second step: Challenge these negative thoughts. Your therapist will teach you how to assess the thoughts that aggravate your anxiety. This is done by evaluating the reality of your fearful thoughts and questioning your irrational attitudes and reactions. To challenge and overcome negative thoughts, you will be advised by your therapist to evaluate the advantages and disadvantages of worrying or having an irrational fear, as well as establishing the accurate probabilities that what makes you anxious will actually happen.

- Third, substitute irrational thoughts with realistic ones. Once you acknowledge your unreasonable expectations and harmful distortions in your apprehensive thoughts, you can switch them with more reasonable, truthful, and progressive thoughts. You will also be taught to use realistic, comforting assertions you can repeat to yourself whenever you face a situation that might stimulate panic or anxiety.

To illustrate how cognitive restructuring works, consider the following example:

Situation: You refuse to go on a rollercoaster because you are afraid you will pass out		
Negative thought: *What if I pass out?!*	Cognitive distortion: Assuming that the worst will happen	Substitute with: I've never passed out, it's more unlikely to happen.
Negative thought: *If I pass out, it'll be too embarrassing!*	Cognitive distortion: Exaggerating	Substitute with: Worst-case scenario, if I pass out, the person next to me will help me out. It'll be just fine!
Negative thought: *Everyone will laugh at me!*	Cognitive distortion: Forming a hasty conclusion	Substitute with: Even if I pass out, my friends will be concerned about me.

Of course, it's not that easy to swap your negative thoughts with more realistic and positive ones. It will take time for it to become a habitual way of thinking. CBT is not fully dependent on your therapist; you will have to do a lot of practice on your own as well.

Exposure Therapy

Anxiety is not easy to deal with alone, especially if it influences your daily life decisions and behaviors. Avoiding the causes of your worries and fears is not a valid solution. For instance, if you have social anxiety, you may refuse an invitation to your friend's wedding. Or if you fear insects, you may not join your friends on a camping trip. Many people who fear heights may take a much longer drive just to avoid going on a tall bridge. This can become very inconvenient and your fears will not only remain, they will become worse.

That's why it's important to expose yourself to situations, concepts, or things that make you fearful or anxious. That's what exposure therapy is all about. The concept of exposure therapy relies on gradual and repeated exposure to your anxiety triggers for the purpose of making you have an improved sense of control over such situations. This way, you are confronting your fears and diminishing your anxiety.

Exposure therapy includes two aspects. You may visualize and imagine the frightening situation (with the help of your therapist), or you may be exposed to it in real life. Exposure therapy may solely be applied, or it may be accompanied by cognitive behavioral therapy.

Exposure therapy depends on systematic desensitization, meaning that it is conducted gradually and slowly to avoid causing a shock or a trauma. It is usually started by a situation that's only slightly intimidating, and this gradually increases. Systematic desensitization helps you to progressively encounter, challenge, and control your fears, hence building up your confidence and strength.

The step-by-step systematic desensitization process comprises three parts:

- **Practicing and acquiring relaxation skills.** With the help of your therapist, you will learn a relaxation technique, such as deep breathing. It's not enough to practice with your therapist, but in order to master this skill, you have to do a lot of work alone. When you get to the stage of confronting your fear, you'll resort to the learned relaxation technique in order to control your anxiety response, such as quivering, sweating, and hyperventilating, and instead manage to relax and take control of the situation.
- **Preparing a step-by-step list.** Your therapist will ask you to prepare a list of scary situations that lead to your final objective. For instance, if your ultimate objective is to overcome your fear of flying, your therapist might start by showing you photos of planes, and you will most probably end up by taking a real flight. Of

course, every step will be specific, clear, and well measured.
- **Taking baby steps.** Also with the help and guidance from your therapist, you'll begin to go through the list, taking it step by step. You will not go to the next step if you haven't conquered your initial fears. This will happen gradually according to your comfort. Whenever your anxiety gets too severe, you will stop to practice the relaxation method you've been taught. After you calm down, you can focus again on the situation. You will take baby steps so you won't feel overwhelmed or distraught.

To illustrate how systematic desensitization works, consider the following example:

Follow the following steps in order to confront and overcome your *cynophobia* (extreme fear of dogs):

1. Lie down or sit in a comfortable position. Breathe deeply and slowly while listening to relaxing music.
2. Once you feel yourself totally relaxed, visualize a dog and imagine yourself getting closer in order to pet it.
3. Visualize how it would feel to pet the dog, focusing on your senses.
4. Look at photos of dogs.
5. Watch a video on dogs.

6. Inspect dogs from a distance, noticing how they can't be harmful.
7. Go to a dog shelter or visit someone that has a dog. If it makes you more comfortable, make sure the dog is on a leash.
8. Be decisive not to panic but to approach the dog.
9. Challenge yourself to stay calm and pet the dog.
10. When you find yourself comfortable enough, spend some time with the dog without the leash.

Can you think of another situation that can be relevant to you? List in the space below the steps you can take to overcome your fear:

Prescribed Medication

Medication doesn't cure anxiety, but it can help you monitor your symptoms. That's why medication is always preferably taken along with therapy.

It's important to discuss the different kinds of available medication. Every person responds differently to medication than others; that's why you should consult repeatedly with your doctor in order to find the best medication to suit you.

Types of Different Anxiety Medication

Benzodiazepines: These are sedative drugs that work on relaxing the muscles and calming the mind. They function by augmenting the impact of the neurotransmitters that relay messages between the brain cells. Benzodiazepines are usually given to patients who suffer from anxiety, particularly generalized anxiety disorder, social anxiety disorder, or panic attacks. Benzodiazepines are usually given by doctors for short-term treatment of anxiety. This is because of the long-term side effects on your balance and memory. Other side effects may include drowsiness, blurred vision, confusion, headaches, and depression. You cannot use these drugs if they are not prescribed to you by your doctor. You also cannot stop using these drugs suddenly, but should consult with your doctor to slowly taper off your dosage to lessen the danger of a seizure.

Examples of benzodiazepines:

- Diazepam (Valium)
- Lorazepam (Ativan)
- Alprazolam (Xanax)
- Chlordiazepoxide (Librium)

Buspirone: This is used to treat both short-term anxiety and chronic anxiety disorders. Buspirone functions by modifying chemicals in the brain that regulate mood, calm anxiety, and decrease the physical symptoms of anxiety; this can take up to a few weeks to show effects. Like any other drug, Buspirone has several disturbing side effects, such as dizziness, nausea, fatigue, insomnia and headaches.

Selective Serotonin Reuptake Inhibitors (SSRIs): These work by raising serotonin levels. Serotonin is a neurotransmitter that influences mood, sexual desire, appetite, sleep, and memory. SSRIs are typically started at a low dose that your doctor gradually increases. SSRIs are a type of antidepressants that can be prescribed to you by your doctor. They also need a few weeks to start showing noticeable effects. However, SSRIs have various side effects, such as nausea, fatigue, lethargy, and sexual dysfunction.

Examples of SSRIs:

- Sertraline (Zoloft)

- Paroxetine (Paxil)

- Escitalopram (Lexapro)

- Fluoxetine (Prozac)

Tricyclics: Tricyclics are given for treatment of all anxiety disorders except obsessive-compulsive disorder (OCD). They function similarly to SSRIs and are also types of antidepressants. Doctors usually initiate tricyclics at a low dose and then gradually increase it. Tricyclics are used less often due to their side effects, especially as the dose is increased. Side effects may include drowsiness, lethargy, dryness in the mouth, nausea, vomiting, blurry vision, and most commonly weight gain.

Examples of tricyclics:

- Doxepin (Sinequan)
- Amitriptyline (Elavil)

Monoamine oxidase inhibitors (MAOIs): MAOIs are prescribed in order to treat social phobia and panic disorder. They function by augmenting neurotransmitters that enhance the mood. MAOIs are not widely used due to their risky side effects and restrictions. There are certain foods that you can't eat if you are taking MAOIs, for example red wine and many types of cheese. Taking other medications and even herbal supplements, such as pain relievers, birth control pills, or allergy drugs, can dangerously react with MAOIs. One of the most severe side effects to MAOIs is an increase in blood pressure level.

Examples of MAOIs:

- Isocarboxazid (Marplan)

- Phenelzine (Nardil)
- Selegiline (Emsam)
- Tranylcypromine (Parnate)

Marijuana and CBD

Marijuana has gained a wide popularity lately due to its relaxation effects; a lot of people are turning to it to manage their anxiety disorders. There isn't enough research to confirm the benefits of cannabis in treating anxiety and depression, yet many cases and scientific reports have reported that it has a palliative effect that eases symptoms of anxiety. However, this kind of self-medication gives an immediate but temporary relief of the distressing anxiety of symptoms, hence causing dependency and reinforcement of its use.

Marijuana may provide a lot of benefits in terms of handling anxiety symptoms, but it is accompanied by many risks as is shown the table below:

Benefits	Risks
• Temporarily reduces depression • Temporarily soothes anxiety	• Increases levels of psychiatric disorders • Forms psychological

symptoms • Reduces stress • Improves sleep	dependence • Affects long-term memory • Increases anxiety symptoms • Causes dependency and increased tolerance and need • May cause cannabis hyperemesis syndrome • Decrease in coordination and focus

CBD and THC

Cannabidiol, or CBD, is one of about 200 cannabinoids found in marijuana plants. It can also be extracted from hemp seeds. CBD is not psychoactive and has a different pharmacologic characteristic than other psychoactive cannabinoids. In other words, it doesn't cause any feelings of intoxication or the 'high' that is usually associated with cannabis. Some research has shown promising results as to CBD relieving anxiety. There isn't enough scientific evidence to confirm the effectiveness of CBD in the treatment of anxiety and depression, but there are lots of existing clinical trials that are assessing the possible benefits of CBD for a variety of disorders, including anxiety disorders.

Tetrahydrocannabinol (THC), on the other hand, is the chemical responsible for most of marijuana's psychological effects. It is the main psychoactive element in cannabis that creates the feeling of being 'high.'

How CBD Works

Our body has many different receptors, which are protein-built chemical structures attached to our cells. These receptors collect signals from various stimuli. Studies reveal that CBD interacts with CB1 and CB2 receptors that are located in the central nervous system and the peripheral nervous system. CBD thus alters serotonin (a neurotransmitter) signals. Serotonin is known to affect our mood and emotions, so not having sufficient serotonin can lead to anxiety and depression.

Is Cannabis Safe?

One study implemented on cannabis consumers showed the following:

- Cannabis drastically reduced symptoms of stress, anxiety, and depression.
- Women showed to have greater drops in anxiety than men did.
- Low THC/high CBD cannabis was found mostly effective in lowering the symptoms of depression.
- High THC/high CBD cannabis was found mostly effective lowering symptoms of stress.
- Treatment of depression by cannabis could worsen depression over a period of time.

The last point is what should be of most concern. Cannabis can indeed alleviate physical pain as well mental worries and fears, but this relief is only temporary. When used for a prolonged period, cannabis can have many negative impacts, such as:

- Dependence or addiction
- Decline in IQ
- Drop in school or work performance
- Distorted thinking and concentration
- Depression
- Showing aggressive behavior
- Relationship problems
- Paranoia
- Disinterest in accomplishing important tasks
- Weight loss or gain

Is CBD Safe?

As for CBD, a modern World Health Organization (WHO) journal revealed that "to date, there is no evidence of recreational use of CBD or any public health-related problems associated with the use of pure CBD" (Hazekamp, 2018). Nevertheless, it's not the pure compound of CBD that is the problem, but the indefinite composition and quality of the products, due to the fact that many products in the market may have contaminated elements.

CBD is generally safe, but some people have reported some side effects such vomiting, tiredness and irritability.

Other Holistic Therapies

The latest surveys show that almost half of the people who suffer from anxiety and depression resort to holistic therapies, mainly because they are fascinated by their integrative approaches. These approaches are not modern, but they've become popular in the last few decades.

Traditional Chinese Medicine

Traditional Chinese Medicine (TCM) emphasizes attaining health and wellbeing through the cultivation of harmony within our lives. Harmony brings physical and mental well-being, while disharmony leads to sickness and collapse.

The TCM method links anxiety problems to disorders of Shan You Si (spirit), that influence the Zang Organs that are responsible for emotions. For example, the Spleen Zang relates to anxiety and intense worry, the Kidney Zang to fear, the Liver Zang to anger, and the Lung Zang to sorrow and grief. If one or more of these Zangs is disrupted, then it'll lead to imbalanced emotions. To clarify, this kind of imbalance or disharmony can affect the Qi (pronounced 'chee'), which is the flow of vital energy. TCM is built on the Chinese notion of Qi and the theory of Yin and Yang, which is the synchronization of all the opposed elements and forces that make up our being. The following are the most prevalent TCM methods:

- **Acupuncture** (inserting very thin needles through the skin at specific points of energy) seeks to repair any disharmony between Yin and Yang. The insertion of needles stimulates the body's own healing to recover its natural balance.
- **Tong Ren Therapy** is another TCM method. It involves healing the energy system using the collective unconscious. Groups of patients sit calmly and collect the healing energy. They all become part of the collective unconscious state which stimulates healing energy of Tong Ren.
- **Committing to a healthy lifestyle and self-help** is also integral to the healing process of both methods.
- **Chinese herbal remedies** have gained a wide acceptance mainly because of their non-toxic nature. These remedies have been used to manage anxiety and to reduce the outcomes of aging. Examples of Chinese herbal remedies include ginseng, licorice root, and cynomorium herb.

Tibetan Medicine

Tibetan medicine includes the practices of Ayurveda, Buddhism, and Chinese medicine combined.

Ayurveda is an ancient Indian natural system of medicine. Ayurveda means the knowledge of life. The concept of Ayurveda indicates that disease is caused due to an imbalanced consciousness, therefore it calls for leading a healthy lifestyle and natural therapies to maintain a healthy balance between the body, mind, spirit, and our surroundings. Ayurveda treatment is initiated by an inner cleansing process and then by a distinct diet, herbal remedies, massage therapy, yoga, and meditation.

The main goal of **Buddhism** is the end of suffering. Anxiety is one form of suffering that disturbs people's lives. While our natural reaction to anxiety is to fight it, Buddhism advises the opposite, which is to accept our feelings and emotions. Buddhist studies state that fighting anxiety can only lead to more anxiety because we tend to fight something that already exists within us. Buddhism believes that the source of anxiety is the mind, or what the Buddhist refer to as the "monkey mind," due to its excessive thinking. We believe the mind, and thus we are easily fooled by it. The mind tricks us by giving us fictional thoughts about the future, lies about the present, and misrepresentations about the past. With this flood of negative thoughts, the "monkey mind" triggers anxiety.

When we feel anxious, we tend to worry about anxiety, and hence we fall into a malicious cycle. Buddhism offers wisdom and practice to ease anxiety; by wisdom, it is meant to fully understand what anxiety is, why it is caused, and how to deal with it. A simple yet powerful concept for Buddhism is that anxiety is pointless. A Buddhist monk named Shantideva says, "If the problem can be solved why worry? If the problem cannot be solved, worrying will do you no good",

(*Buddhism | The Cure for Anxiety?*, 2019). If you face a problem that you can solve, then focus your mind and energy on it in the present and work on it; if the problem cannot be solved, then you need to drop it and move on. It's completely useless to waste time and energy worrying about problems that we cannot solve or control. Our irrational thoughts are related to problems that we cannot solve; that's why they are out of our control. Thus, it is vain to constantly worry about them. The Buddhist practice of healing anxiety emphasizes 'dissolvement' rather than 'resolvement.' This is achieved by mindful meditation, in which you focus on the present moment and dissolve the unnecessary thoughts. This method appeases the monkey mind through acceptance and not struggle.

Hypnotherapy

Hypnotherapy is practiced when a patient is in a trance, or a transformed state of consciousness. During hypnosis, a patient is profoundly relaxed, deeply fixated, and vulnerable to susceptibility. That's how hypnosis focuses attention to behaviors that need to be changed. Positive affirmations are provided by the hypnotist, such as "You no longer feel anxious" or "You can control your stress."

According to research, hypnotherapy can aid in relieving anxiety, coping with the symptoms of panic disorder and phobias, and conquering limiting behaviors.

Often, treatment implicates teaching the patient self-hypnosis, which permits the patient to apply this method alone.

Aromatherapy

Research shows that aromatherapy can immediately improve mood and alleviate anxiety. Involving the use of essential oils, it is a safe and effective method for the treatment of anxiety and depression. Essential oils are distilled from plants and are absorbed by the body through the skin pores. This could be applied through a massage or smelling. The scents from the essential oils affect the hypothalamus, a part of the brain that regulates the hormonal system.

Aromatherapy provides instant benefits, such as:
- Lifting up the mood
- Feeling of tranquility and positivity

- Feeling more energized
- Boosting metabolism
- Alleviating stress level
- Generating vivid memory

Common essential oils include lavender, chamomile, jasmine, basil, sage, rose, lemon, frankincense, and peppermint. The responses towards these scents are highly linked to individual preferences.

Aromatherapy is safe, simple, and affordable. You can practice it alone at home in different ways:

- Add the essential oils to an infuser and allow it to fill the room with a soothing scent.
- Add a few drops of essential oils in about two cups of water and stir well. Dip in a cotton washcloth and use it to wipe your hands, face, and neck. You can also store the cloth in a sealed container in the fridge for later use.
- Use scented lotion on your skin made from the suggested or preferred essential oils.
- Keep a scented stick in your pocket and smell it whenever you feel stressed.
- Burn naturally scented incense and let the aroma fill your home.

Botanical Remedies

St John's Wort (Hypericum perforatum)

St. John's wort has been tested clinically and shown to be an effective alternative to SSRIs or tricyclic antidepressants for the treatment of anxiety and depression. However, there are some side effects to this botanical, although their rate is lower than the side effects of prescribed medication. The side effects may include nausea, skin rash, and/or sexual dysfunction.

Valerian

Valerian seems to act like a sedative on the brain and the nervous system. It works as a calmative agent and tranquilizer, especially as a sleep aid. It is believed that valerian may relieve symptoms of anxiety or depression. Despite its benefits, valerian may have some side effects that include headache, stomach ache, and even insomnia.

Rhodiola Rosea (also known as arctic root or golden root)

Rhodiola is a herb that has been used for centuries. It grows in the cold, mountainous areas of Asia and Europe.

Its roots contain more than 140 active ingredients and are considered adaptogens, meaning they help the body acclimate to stress. Rhodiola is consumed as a remedy for anxiety, tiredness, and depression, as well as a nutritional supplement. It has gained popularity, especially in Scandinavian countries, for its multiple mental and physical health benefits that include the following:

- Increases the body's resistance to stress
- Fights fatigue
- Increases body's energy and stamina
- Reduces symptoms of anxiety and depression
- Increases mental performance

Ashwagandha (Withania somnifera)

This plant is found in India and North Africa and has been used for over 3,000 years for the treatment of several illnesses. It's classified as an adaptogen, indicating that it can help your body manage stress and adapt well to it. Ashwagandha extracts or powder are used to treat anxiety and depression specifically, along with other conditions.

Modern science endorses its health benefits in managing and reducing stress and anxiety. It also regulates the mood, alleviates depression, aids in sleep, improves the memory, and can boost brain function.

Ashwagandha is generally safe, but it's advised to consult with your doctor before taking this supplement.

Kava Kava

Kava grows in tropical environments; it's a shrub with green, heart-shaped leaves. Kava has become popular lately for it provides pleasurable sensations and has a soothing, calming effect. Due to its relaxing qualities, kava has caught the attention of the scientists as a potential treatment for generalized anxiety disorder. Its main ingredient is kavain, and scientists have found that it regulates mood and alleviates anxiety symptoms.

Though kava has a lot of health benefits, there are some risks that are associated with it, especially liver injury. Also, some reports show some negative reactions if taken with antianxiety or antidepressant drugs, as well as Parkinson's medication. Kava is usually mixed with hot drinks and should never be mixed with alcohol.

Chapter 7:

Closing Reflection

Testimonial

The following is a real life testimonial from a patient, aged 37, who suffers from different anxiety disorders:

My journey with anxiety started at an early age, around puberty. I was not diagnosed with anxiety then and I had no idea what it meant. Anxiety manifested itself in the form of an illness, which was later diagnosed as Cyclic Vomiting Syndrome (CVS). Almost every month, I was hospitalized due to sudden yet continuous vomiting and extreme abdominal pain, which were also accompanied by severe panic attacks. This situation kept going for years until a time came when I was locked in the psychiatry section for two weeks. My panic attacks kept going, and no matter what medication I was given, once their effect was gone, I was back to panicking and vomiting. I was 26 at the time, and that's when I was diagnosed with panic disorder, generalized anxiety disorder, and PTSD. I had few therapy sessions, but I found them useless. The doctor prescribed me Paxil, and it worked great on me for a few years. However, due to the multiple stressors in my life, I went back to the psychiatry unit with continuous panic attacks. The doctor changed my medication to Seroxat CR and so far, it is working well for me.

But medication doesn't help alone; I've learned different breathing techniques that I practice on a daily basis. I've also changed my lifestyle, which was pretty unhealthy. I dodged junk food and incorporated more proteins and nutrients into my diet. I work out once a week, though I should exercise more often, but I do practice mindful meditation every day, which helps me get a good night's sleep.

I have also tried smoking cannabis, and though it had immediate effect in easing my anxiety symptoms, after a few months I found myself totally dependent on it to lift up my mood. My anxiety got worse, and I lost control over my life. My friends intervened as they saw a lot of negative changes happen to me. I was withdrawn, lethargic, and feeling down most of the time. It wasn't easy dealing with the withdrawal symptoms, especially that it made me more anxious.

I found my escape in writing journals. This helped me recognize my triggers, go back down memory lane, and confront my traumas. Often through my life, I've found myself drowning in a deep dark ocean. I found it hard to talk about my feelings to anyone, basically because most of the time I didn't comprehend exactly what I was feeling. Depression and anxiety completely took hold of me, and I found myself surrendering to them. I used to think that what you feel is ignited by immediate triggers, but I had to get back to the roots of my problems and traumas to understand and acknowledge them.

I live in a country that has never been politically or economically stable. I've lived through four wars, and I believe that that has taken the worst toll on me. I was drastically traumatized as a child due to the daily bombings. I could only describe my childhood as fearful and insecure. In addition to that, I was repeatedly sexually harassed by three different men. This made my teenage years unbearable, for I secluded myself from everyone and my separation anxiety started to show. At the age of 16, I met my first boyfriend. I finally gained confidence and strength, but a year after he passed away due to drug overdose. That's when I first experienced loss in my life. Losing someone close to me left me shattered, and I had to pick up the pieces again. My family also played a huge role in increasing my anxiety. Living in poverty didn't have much impact, for it taught me to work hard to earn a living. However, my parents' constant fighting negatively and significantly impacted me. My house was not a home; it wasn't a safe haven. I was in constant worry that something might happen to my mom or siblings. Even when my siblings grew up and started their own families, I was still continuously worried about them.

I remember one time when I was at the hospital, a psychologist asked me why I was so anxious. I told her that I have the excessive fear that something might happen to my family. She then asked about my family, where they were and how they were doing. When I said that they were living their lives as they should be, I realized that I was the only one suffering. It made me realize that my thoughts were irrational. That's why I started practicing mindful meditation and focused on the present moment. I recited positive affirmations every morning and every night to keep myself strong and optimistic.

One thing that really helped me was setting goals. I was determined to change my life, accept new challenges, and enjoy the rewards. I excelled at my work and placed most of my focus on developing my career as a high school teacher. My interactions with my colleagues and students made me more outgoing and social. Setting goals is absolutely effective because it always gave me something to look forward to.

I've adopted some mottos, like "This too shall pass," "What you think is what you feel," etc. I've also come up with my own motto:

"Happiness is like a mirage, you can't chase after it, you need to create it." Find yourself a motto and keep it in your mind when things get tough. Positive affirmations are really helpful, especially if you start your day with them.

My advice to anyone who suffers from anxiety or depression is to keep moving on. Never give up, never feel sorry for yourself, and never allow yourself to be pitiful. If there's a problem, work on solving it. There's nothing you can not do. When you need help, don't hesitate to ask for it. You will need help so seek it, yet be confident that you are the best therapist. If you don't help yourself, nothing and no one will be able to help you overcome your struggles. Life isn't easy, but it's not impossible; if we set our minds rightfully, then we can lead a positive and contented life.

Setting Your Goals

Studies show that setting positive, achievable goals is effective in the treatment of anxiety and depression. Psychologists from different renowned universities such as the University of Liverpool, Edith Cowan University, and the University of Exeter examined the connection between anxiety and depression and setting and pursuing individual goals (*Could More Effective Goals Be the Key to Treating Depression?*, n.d.). The research observed 42 individuals who suffer from anxiety and depression who established personal goals and another 51 with no history of anxiety or depression. Both groups planned their approach and avoidance goals. Approach goals mainly concentrate on attaining a desired target, for instance mastering playing the guitar.

Avoidance goals, on the other hand, concentrate on avoiding an undesired result, for example avoiding drinking alcohol when stressed.

The study revealed that those suffering from depression were as motivated as those without depression. Both groups set a comparable number of goals and regarded their individual equally. Nonetheless, those who experience depression were less optimistic about accomplishing their goals and found it harder to generate goals with positive results. They were more prone to relinquish goals that they perceived as unfeasible.

Associate Professor Dickson stated, "While disengaging from unattainable goals is thought to help break a cycle of goal failure, negative thinking and depression this is complicated by the difficulty in setting new goals for people with depression. If we can develop better ways to help people with depression set goals that are achievable and focused on positive outcomes, and assist them in identifying ways to achieve their goals, it is likely to enhance a sense of well-being. Personal goals are integral to many therapies such as Cognitive Behavior Therapy and Behavior Activation Therapy used to treat depression. Therefore, a better understanding of personal goal processes shows promise in developing more effective treatments for depression" (*Could More Effective Goals Be the Key to Treating Depression?*, n.d.).

Goals are essential in life for they drive us forward. It's fundamental that you understand the importance of setting goals and employ this understanding in your daily life. According to Professor Dickson, the confidence built around setting goals provides an effective method in reducing anxiety and depression.

14 Reasons Why Focused Goal Setting Is Important:

- You employ your abilities and talents on something useful
- Gives you a sense of direction
- Provides a concrete endpoint to aim for
- Focuses your mind on a specific target
- Enables you to measure your progress
- Sets mental boundaries for yourself
- Keeps you away from distractions as your goal remains in focus
- Raises self-confidence and self-care
- Makes you accountable for attaining specific goals
- Helps you overcome procrastination and laziness as your set time limits
- Motivates and inspires you as they provide a foundation for your drive
- Helps you organize your time and resources to achieve something beneficial
- Offers you a sense of meaning and purpose
- Provides you with a happy, satisfied, and proud feeling

How to Set Your Goals

Follow these steps to achieve your goals:

- **Decide on setting a goal that you like or find desirable.** It should be something you're interested in or feel enthusiastic about, something that you do for your own sake and not for anyone else. It's better if you start with smaller things and gradually aim for bigger goals.
- **Break your goal down.** If you aim high, it's a good idea to break down your goal into smaller aims as steps to achieving your end goal. Make sure your steps are clear, specified, and feasible. For example, if your goal is to change your lifestyle and make it healthier, specify what aspects in your life you want to change. Your smaller aim could be starting to exercise every morning for 15 minutes and gradually increase it every day. Another step could be to eliminate sodas and junk food. Clear and specific goals will help you attain your bigger goal, especially since you will feel a sense of accomplishment whenever you fulfill a step.
- **Write down your goal.** Writing down your goals holds you accountable for them. It also helps you measure your progress and keep you focused. Visualize how you'd feel once you accomplish your goal and write that down as

well. This will keep you motivated and determined to reach your end goal.
- **Share your goal with someone close to you.** This will encourage you to stick to your goals as you receive more incentive from others. It would also be great if you and your partner work together towards achieving a common goal.
- **Carefully decide on your first step.** Jeff Galloway (2017) once said, "A lifestyle change begins with a vision and a single step." Visualize the bigger picture and be decisive on taking the first step. If you have the courage to take the first step, then you will have the courage to persist and reach your aspiration.
- **Be persistent.** Of course, it won't be all easy; you will face some bumps, but the most important thing is to keep going. If you find yourself stuck at a stage, take a break or look for something else and keep going. If you struggle, you can always seek help from those around you for they may help you perceive things differently. Considering things from different perspectives will help succeed in reaching your goals.
- **Reward yourself.** When you succeed in achieving your goal, praise yourself and allow yourself to celebrate your accomplishment. Reflect on the highs and lows of your journey and give yourself a pat on the back.

- **Set your mind on your next goal.** Now is the best time to keep going and accomplishing new things in your life. If you feel fulfilled and gratified with what you've achieved, challenge yourself with new goals. Learn something new, something that you've never thought of doing before, like learning a new language or playing a musical instrument.

Self-Reflection is Vital for a Positive Attitude

Self-reflection is very important because it can help you alter your mindset, expand positivity in your life, and create a better connection with yourself.

Self-reflection helps you to understand ways that you respond to critical situations, identify your weaknesses, and find ways that you can deal with situations in a positive way instead of letting them overwhelm you.

Self-reflection is the practice of transporting your attention to what's happening in your life in a mindful and progressive way.

Self-reflection is mainly about building self-awareness. So many of us focus on moving forward and getting things done without taking the needed time to reflect on our internal thoughts and feelings.

There are many ways to apply self-reflection, but the most effective method is through writing.

Make self-reflection a priority in your life because it:
- Helps make better sense of things
- Makes you recognize your strengths and weaknesses
- Urges you to find solutions to your problems
- Helps you challenge negative and irrational thoughts
- Makes you accept change and trace your progress
- Improves self-awareness
- Encourages self-acceptance
- Inspires you to live with a purpose

Reflection Chart

After trying the different methods to help you calm and cope with your anxiety, refer to the following chart to reflect on your progress. Follow the first example provided as a guide.

Methods that work best to calm your anxiety	Changes that you've done that improved your lifestyle	Other changes that you need to do	Your upcoming goals!

breathing techniques	exercising and becoming more active	change my diet	participate in a public speaking contest

Conclusion

A Preventative Protection Plan

This book aims at teaching you to find cognitive, emotive, and behavior methods to overcome tormenting anxieties and fears. This process is built by your mind power, creative power, and will power. You need to have a preventative protection plan to avoid relapsing or going back to previous habits that cause you anxiety. The following is an example of a preventative protection plan:

Prevention Factor	Mind power	Creative power	Will power
Cognitive	Realize your anxious thoughts and fears when they first start to spark.	Sustain a healthy perception by recognizing and questioning these conflicts. Think of other ways to tackle these clashes.	Focus on your main motivations for stopping anxieties and fears from returning. How important are these motivations?

Emotive acceptance	Recognize the emotional impact of your anxious thoughts. If you find yourself having the urge to withdraw, can you find a better way to control your thoughts?	Find adaptive methods to acknowledge and accept the distress caused by your anxiety. Form a positive adaptive visualization of yourself coping with the problem that is causing you discomfort. Determine to translate your visualization into action.	Find the will to accept, confront, and face your problem. If it's causing you to feel fearful, what coping methods will you apply to deal with it?
Behavior	Identify what behaviors accompany your anxious thoughts and emotions. What can you do to defy them? Will you avoid this fear or work	What actions will you take to protect yourself from negative thoughts? How will you maintain your positivity?	Can determination and persistence help you cope with and overcome your anxiety? How will you benefit from that?

	on conquering it?		

Now it's your turn to create your own preventative protection plan, specifying the cognitive, emotive acceptance, and behavior methods that you will follow, along with your mind, creativity, and will power to control your worries and fear. Make sure to put your plan into action.

Prevention Factor	Mind power	Creative power	Will power
Cognitive			
Emotive acceptance			

Behavior			

Final Word

We hope that you've found the help you were looking for in this book. Continue practicing the suggested methods and techniques that you've found helpful in the future to maintain your mental, emotional, and physical well-being. If you feel that your anxiety is getting way out of control, it's advisable to seek professional help. Do not use any medication without consulting your doctor and getting the right prescribed medicine to your case.

Once you've tried all the different suggested approaches to calm your anxiety, go back to the anxiety quiz presented in the introduction to measure your progress.

Keep in mind that self-improvement takes time and you have to be patient. Focus on the big picture and enjoy the present moment. Stay mindful and closely observe the changes you go through. Enjoy the rewards that you receive. Keep setting goals and challenges for yourself; there's always more room for self-improvement. Help others by sharing what you've learned and contribute to the well-being of those around you. Don't settle to just be satisfied, aim to thrive!

References

9 Bad Habits of People With Anxiety. (n.d.). The Mighty. https://themighty.com/2018/03/bad-habit-anxiety

Activedia. "Spiritualism Awakening Meditation." Pixabay, pixabay.com/photos/spiritualism-awakening-meditation-4552237/. Accessed 12 Sept. 2020.

Ayurveda. 2019, www.hopkinsmedicine.org/health/wellness-and-prevention/ayurveda. Accessed 17 Sept. 2020.

Black, D. S., O'Reilly, G. A., Olmstead, R., Breen, E. C., & Irwin, M. R. (2015). Mindfulness Meditation and Improvement in Sleep Quality and Daytime Impairment Among Older Adults With Sleep Disturbances. *JAMA Internal Medicine*, *175*(4), 494. https://doi.org/10.1001/jamainternmed.2014.8081

Buddhism | The Cure for Anxiety? (2019, April 24). Einzelgänger. https://einzelganger.co/buddhism-the-cure-for-anxiety/

Cottonbro. "Couple Having A Misunderstanding." Pexels, www.pexels.com/photo/couple-having-a-misunderstanding-3692885/. Accessed 19 Sept. 2020.

Depression *and Caregiving | Family Caregiver Alliance*. (2020). Caregiver.Org. https://www.caregiver.org/depression-and-caregiving

Desmaisons, K. (1999). Potatoes not prozac : a natural seven-step dietary plan to control your cravings and lose weight, recognize how foods affect the way you feel, and stabilize the level of sugar in your blood. Simon & Schuster.

Dezalb. "Flower Valerian Inflorescence." Pixabay, pixabay.com/photos/flower-valerian-inflorescence-5399562/. Accessed 18 Sept. 2020.

Galloway, J. (2017). "Jeff Galloway: Your Personal Running Journal: Logging Your Progress, Keeping Your Motivation", p.38, Meyer & Meyer Sport

George, F. (2017, January). (PDF) Stress: Concepts, Definition and History. ResearchGate. https://www.researchgate.net/publication/312003144_Stress_Concepts_Definition_and_History

Glycemic index diet: What's behind the claims. (2017). Mayo Clinic. https://www.mayoclinic.org/healthy-lifestyle/nutrition-and-healthy-eating/in-depth/glycemic-index-diet/art-20048478

Hain, John. "Woman Profile Recycle." Pixabay, pixabay.com/illustrations/woman-profile-recycle-remember-1000769/. Accessed 12 Sept. 2020.

Hazekamp, Arno. "The Trouble with CBD Oil." Medical Cannabis and Cannabinoids, vol. 1, no. 1, 12 June 2018, pp. 65–72, www.karger.com/Article/FullText/489287, 10.1159/000489287. Accessed 15 Sept. 2020.

Kind, Shelley. "Can Mindfulness Really Help Reduce Anxiety?" Anxiety.Org, 10 Nov. 2014, www.anxiety.org/can-mindfulness-help-reduce-anxiety. Accessed 12 Sept. 2020.

Mayo Clinic Staff. (2019, March 19). *Chronic stress puts your health at risk*. Mayo Clinic. https://www.mayoclinic.org/healthy-lifestyle/stress-management/in-depth/stress/art-20046037

Mareefe. "Two Clear Glass Bottles With Liquids." Pexels, www.pexels.com/photo/two-clear-glass-bottles-with-liquids-672051/. Accessed 17 Sept. 2020.

Monicore. "Succulent Flowers Colors." Pixabay, pixabay.com/photos/succulent-flowers-colors-plant-2412436/. Accessed 18 Sept. 2020.

Office of Dietary Supplements - Zinc. (2016). Nih.Gov. https://ods.od.nih.gov/factsheets/Zinc-HealthProfessional/

Peggychoucair. "Break Time Out Worker." Pixabay, pixabay.com/photos/break-time-out-workers-hand-beer-4073387/. Accessed 18 Sept. 2020.

Peter, D., & Gazelle, H. (2017). Anxious Solitude and Self-Compassion and Self-Criticism Trajectories in Early Adolescence: Attachment Security as a Moderator. Child Development, 88(6), 1834–1848. https://doi.org/10.1111/cdev.12926

Piacquadio, A. (n.d.). Photo of Sleeping Man. Www.Pexels.Com. Retrieved September 7, 2020, from https://www.pexels.com/photo/photo-of-sleeping-man-3771069/

PhotoMIX-Company. "Herb St John'S Wort Flower Closeup." Pixabay, pixabay.com/photos/herb-st-john-s-wort-flower-closeup-1541346/. Accessed 18 Sept. 2020.

Phuong, Le Minh. "Woman Meditating on Wooden Dock." Unsplash,

unsplash.com/photos/niH7Z81S44g. Accessed 12 Sept. 2020.

Read, R. N. P. A. N. E. L. updated: 4 M. 2020 ~ 3 min. (2020, March 4). Unhealthy Diet Linked to Anxiety Disorders. Psychcentral.Com. https://psychcentral.com/news/2020/03/04/unhealthy-diet-linked-to-anxiety-disorders/154542.html

Separation Anxiety | Encyclopedia.com. (2019). Encyclopedia.Com. https://www.encyclopedia.com/medicine/psychology/psychology-and-psychiatry/separation-anxiety#3447200510

Shevtsova, D. (n.d.). Woman in White Lace Cap. Www.Pexels.Com. Retrieved September 7, 2020, from https://www.pexels.com/photo/woman-in-white-lace-cap-sleeved-top-and-green-skirt-hiding-behind-brown-wall-1030982/

Steimer, T. (2002). The biology of fear- and anxiety-related behaviors. Dialogues in Clinical Neuroscience, 4(3), 231–249. https://www.ncbi.nlm.nih.gov/pmc/articles/PMC3181681/

Suni, E. (2019). Don't Let Anxiety Or Stress Keep You Up All Night Counting Sheep- National Sleep Foundation. Sleepfoundation.Org. https://www.sleepfoundation.org/articles/how-does-anxiety-affect-sleep

Teichmann, Julia. "Cbd Kapsein Cannabidiol Hemp." Pixabay, pixabay.com/photos/cbd-cbd-kapseln-cannabidiol-4474903/. Accessed 15 Sept. 2020.

Telling Others About Your Anxiety | ADAVIC Anxiety Disorders Association of Victoria, Inc. (n.d.). Www.Adavic.Org.Au. https://www.adavic.org.au/PG-articles-telling-others-about-your-anxiety.aspx

TheDigitalArtist. (n.d.). Stress Anxiety Depression. Pixabay. Retrieved September 10, 2020, from https://pixabay.com/photos/stress-anxiety-depression-unhappy-2902537/

Therapy | Anxiety and Depression Association of America, ADAA. (2019). Adaa.Org. https://adaa.org/finding-help/treatment/therapy

These Bad Habits Make My Anxiety Worse. (2019, November 21). Healthline. https://www.healthline.com/health/anxiety-relapses-the-temptation-of-bad-habits

"This Is Why Deep Breathing Makes You Feel so Chill." Right as Rain by UW Medicine, RightAsRain, 4 June 2018, rightasrain.uwmedicine.org/mind/stress/why-deep-breathing-makes-you-feel-so-chill. Accessed 11 Sept. 2020.

Tumiso. "Loneliness Crown Depression." Pixabay, pixabay.com/photos/loneliness-crowd-depression-sad-4785245/. Accessed 17 Sept. 2020.

University of Liverpool. "Could More Effective Goals Be the Key to Treating Depression?" Medicalxpress.Com, medicalxpress.com/news/2016-12-effective-goals-key-depression.html. Accessed 18 Sept. 2020.

www.ingramcontent.com/pod-product-compliance
Lightning Source LLC
LaVergne TN
LVHW040059080526
838202LV00045B/3714